GIVE ME TEN DAYS

GIVE ME TEN DAYS

CANDACE PARKER

Give Me Ten Days
Copyright © 2020 by Candace Parker
All rights reserved

No portion of this book may be reproduced, stored in a retrieval system, or transmitted in any form by any means–electronic, mechanical, photocopy, recording, or other except for brief quotations in printed reviews, without prior permission of the author.

Claire Aldin Publications www.clairealdin.com

First Edition
Printed in the United States

Paperback ISBN: 978-1-9542740-0-6
eBook ISBN: 978-1-7349969-9-9

*This book is dedicated to Dreamer and Stay Woke.
Through your friendship, I have found true sisterhood.*

PART 1

PROLOGUE

ONE YEAR AGO

Tale as old as time
True as it can be
Barely even friends
Then somebody bends
Unexpectedly

"I have to be honest with you. I can't do this anymore." Charms' words echoed in my head. But, I'm getting ahead of myself. Charm is the guy I met two years ago. Our meeting went a little like this:

"Candace," someone at church said touching my arm, "I want to introduce you." I turned around. "This is ******." *Side note, Reader: For the purpose of this story, I'm referring to the man in question as "Charm," as in, "he charmed the birds off the trees."* Okay, back to it.

We were standing close to the altar after service, everyone chatting and catching up. All the other bodies seemed to disappear so that it was just this gorgeous man and me.

He leaned in, and took my hand in an enveloping grip. "Charm," he said in a deep voice.

"I'm Candace, it's nice to meet you…" I was confused — I would've known if he were a regular attendee. I'd have noticed him. "So you are new?"

"Yes, actually, some of my extended family used to go here. I moved so I could be closer to school, so this is my new church."

"School?"

"University of Michigan. Studying business. Also play basketball."

Dang. This man was painfully good-looking, warm, shining eyes, tall broad-shouldered. Even his style was clean, sharp, but not preppy. A lot of these Michigan boys go for that golfer, business casual look. Not this guy. His suit fit him perfectly.

"Well in that case," I gave him a playful smile and an appropriate church greeting. What, I was just being friendly, right?

We chatted. He talked about himself a bit. This guy was a catch, and he knew it. Mmm-hmm.

"Are you from Detroit?" he asked.

"Yes, I am. Got my degree here as well."

"What did you study?"

"Social work. But I'm not a social worker. I mean, I do 'social' work, but mostly through the church."

"Alright," he smiled again, "I guess even right now with this conversation you are technically doing 'social' work." That made me laugh. I went on to explain that I work at a bank, and I'm also a writer.

"A writer?" This got his attention. "You write books?"

"No, I haven't written a whole book yet, mostly blogging and articles in magazines, stuff like that."

Little did he or I know that in my future book, he would feature as a main character.

But let's get back to the day when everything changed.

Charm: Any plans tonight?

Me: Nah.

Charm: You want to catch that movie?

Me: Which one?

Charm: That horror movie. "Don't Breathe."

Me: Oh right, they filmed it here in Detroit, right?

Charm: Yeah, it looks good. There's a 7:15.

Me: Sure, let's do it.

Charm: I'll pick you up.

An hour later, his truck pulled up to my stoop. I had on no make-up, a grey hoodie, leggings and Uggs.

I climbed into the truck, and he gave me a hug.

"Hey."

"Hey, Beautiful. You didn't have to get all dressed up. It's just the movies."

"What, this old thing?" I pointed to my Michigan State hoodie. We laughed and he pulled away from the curb.

I had to laugh at him calling me "Beautiful." That's what he called me every time, like it was my nickname. We talked on the way there, about the week, about the position opening up at his new job and how he wanted to go for it. I told him I would look at his resume if he wanted my help. He said he would really appreciate that.

We got to the empty theater and got Milk Duds and popcorn.

The lights dimmed, and as the trailers started, Charm moved the armrest between us out of the way. I thought he did it to put the popcorn between us, but instead, he inched toward me. I felt the heat coming off him. During scary scenes, I would jump, and Charm would reach over and give my arm a reassuring squeeze.

On the way home, we talked about the movie, how it was cool to see your own hometown on the screen, but maybe not in a horror film. "I'm going to be scared going through some of those neighborhoods now!" I protested.

"I'll get you a baseball bat to carry in your purse," he joked.

In our usual routine, Charm would drop me off. But that night, he pulled his truck up to the curb and killed the engine.

"Weeknight," I reminded him, yawning.

"I know, I just, I have something I want to talk to you about."

"Okay," I turned toward him, expecting to hear more about his family, or school or some other conundrum.

"I have to be honest with you. I can't do this anymore." I jumped, just like I did in the theater.

"Do what?"

"This friendship thing."

My heart thundered in my chest. "You don't want to be friends anymore?" I couldn't keep the high pitch out of my voice.

"No, it's —" he struggled for words. And then he finally started talking in a rush. "I think about you all day. I see you in church, I can't pay attention to the sermon because I can't take my eyes off of you." Fourteen different emotions bubbled through me. He kept going, "My family loves you, and I've watched you date all these other dudes that don't get you. I want a chance. Don't I deserve a chance?"

I felt light-headed, confused, shocked even. I had done so much work to build this friendship with him, to get to this safe place with him, and I had told him all my secrets.

He waited, his eyes searching mine. "Candace, if it doesn't work out, we still have our friendship."

I managed to come to my senses and think rationally for a second. "But you said, 'I can't do this anymore,' like I have to choose between being your friend and being your girlfriend?"

"I didn't mean it like that," he soft peddled, but it sure did feel like an ultimatum. "I just think we can make this work. And I want to. I want you."

The facade of friendship came crashing down the moment he kissed me that night in the truck; the warmth of his lips flooded my whole body with a tingling potion. He cupped my face in his hands. I put my hands on his wrists.

This was what I had dreamed of my whole girlhood. A man who really knew me, and loved me for just being me. It felt safe, it felt right. Something in me broke loose, like a dam that had been holding back a river.

Cue the music:
Just a little change
Small to say the least
Both a little scared
Neither one prepared
Beauty and the beast

THREE MONTHS AGO

I barely can concentrate at work because I'm staring at a dozen roses that are meant to make up for the following exchange:

> Me: Earth to Charm… *(A day goes by)*
> Me: Hey, is everything okay? *(Two hours go by)*
> Me: Charm, I'm starting to worry. Please just txt me back and let me know you are okay, and you are just busy?

The next day:

    Charm: Hey Beautiful. I've just been really busy with school, and work, all that. How are you?

    Me: Really? I was worried. You can't even just text me back and let me know?

    Charm: Oh here we go. Why do you need to know where I am every single moment of the day?

    Me: It's been 4 days.

    Charm: Why are you so paranoid?

    Me: I'm sorry, what?

    Charm: Why do you always have to assume the worst?

    Me (in a huff but wanting to resolve): I'm glad you're okay.

One hour goes by.

    Charm: Can I see you tonight?

    Charm: Candace?

    Charm: So, you're not even going to answer my phone call?

Two can play at that game, I thought, after ignoring three of his calls. The long glass vase sitting on my desk with a handwritten card that reads, *I love you,* reminded me of how persistent he can be. And how much I like it.

At least Charm tried to make it right when he messed up, unlike some of my other boyfriends. He may go AWOL for a couple days at a time and nearly give me a coronary, but at least he follows up with roses and an apology. I read somewhere that when men feel vulnerable, they will withdraw because they "need space." Is that what he's doing, and that's why he circles back with a bouquet?

Charm follows that same non-committal pattern, but he responds to my freakout differently. The more I push him away, the tighter he holds on.

It's refreshing to know I'm wanted. They *are* really pretty roses.

THREE WEEKS AGO

Me: I haven't heard from you in days. We have to talk about these Paris tickets — are we still going? I need to confirm this with work if I'm going to take the time off.

Eight hours later.

Me: We are going to lose those reservations if we don't lock it down by tomorrow.

The next day.

Me: Charm?

CHAPTER 1

WEDNESDAY

7:21 A.M.
I'm in my bathrobe looking down at my phone. The screen says: *This isn't working out. We should just move on.* My breathing starts to rush, like I'm getting ready for a fight. It feels like all the blood in my body is draining out of me. What type of sicko dumps a person on a Wednesday? Someone with no morals, that's who.

Oh I'm pissed now, pacing the floor in my little apartment. This really messes up my schedule. I mean, at least if I got dumped on a Monday, I'd be too preoccupied with work, and if he had waited for the weekend like a decent person, I'd have two days to keen and sleep, call my girlfriends and vent. But no. This jerk just had to throw off my week. Again, no morals. Clearly this relationship was doomed to fail anyway.

Wednesday: the night of Bible Study, where we've gone together every Wednesday night for nearly the last two years. The place where he spoke so eloquently that several parishioners suggested he become a minister?

Alright, I admit to myself as I climb in the hottest shower I can stand, it's not the day of the week that is making me furious: It's that I didn't dump him on Tuesday. Actually, I should have dumped him after he said we should "chill" on the Paris idea. What am I going to do about that half-paid ticket? Grrrr.

I flashback to our texts yesterday:

Me: Hey? Where are you?
(Two hours later)
Me: Why are you ghosting me?
Charm: I'm not. I have studying, a full-time job, I'm hustling all day, everyday. You wouldn't understand.
Me: How am I supposed to know any of that if you haven't answered any of my texts or calls for three days?
Charm: Look, you need to chill. I had some stuff going on, but it's not really your business, it doesn't affect you.
Me: ?

Who says that to the person they love? Why didn't I just cut him loose on Tuesday?

7:37 A.M.

I scrub myself in the shower as though I can wash that man right off me. If I had dumped him, the rest of my week would have been righteous. I'd blaze into work singing, "This girl is on Fiiiiiirrrreeeee!" Victorious. Why didn't I just dump him? I should have seen this coming a mile away. Why didn't I cut it off at the pass? Lord knows what he is doing when he goes silent for days at a time, but he's not studying, that's for sure.

The water is pouring down my face, steam coming off me. I get soap in my eyes, and the sting feels the same as my stinging ego. If only I had admitted to myself that he was not the man I thought he was. I should have trusted my first impression…well, second:

Him: What's your name again? (Looking me up and down.)

Me: My name is "you should've remembered it" (Laughing.)

Him: Come on, don't be like that. I'm a good guy, you should get to know me, Candace.

Ouch, another red flag. Note to self: Guys don't have to go around saying "I'm a good guy" if they are *actually* good guys…even if they do remember your name.

He was playing a long game, and right now, he's thinking that he won. How dare he dump ME. I point out that he cancelled our last three dates and this is what he does? He tosses a year and a half in the garbage. I let out a huge frustrated growl that echoes in the shower.

8:02 A.M.
Business casual is a dress and boots for me because it takes less thought. I brush my hair, which I have worn the same for years: long and straight with a part in the middle to go with my cat-eye glasses. It's my thing. I put on my makeup, gather my things.

I give Charlie a quick spin around the block so he can do his business and deliver him back to my place. He's my Shorkie, a Shi-Tzu Yorkshire Terrier cross. He's grey and white and smiles like a person. Right now, he is giving me a look like, "Aw, you're leaving? Again? You call that a walk?" Even though this is how we do it every day.

"Yes, Buddy. I'll see you tonight. Be good, okay?"

It's breezy and chilly outside, and a new wave of outrage hits me like a gust of wind coming off the lake. Should've brought my jacket.

My boots clack on the pavement as I march down the sidewalk toward my vehicle.

Inside my head I'm yelling: *I'm the best thing that's ever happened to him! Being with me will forever be his greatest accomplishment! Wait until he realizes what a big mistake he's made! I feel sorry for the chick that dates him after me! She better brace herself every Wednesday!*

The blood is rising in my face as I stump to my car. It's cold out this morning, but I feel hot. Furiously hot.

He sure did have some moves. Three steps ahead of me. Even used my body against me. When he lowered his voice and just took my hand, it felt too good to say no. I mean, I did say no to, you know. From the beginning, I was clear about not wanting to get down before marriage. But that was part of the chase for him, wasn't it, to see if he could get me to break my own rules?

Still, we had these moments of genuine closeness. At times, the chemistry was so intense, our makeout sessions had me considering throwing in the towel. All he had to do was call and say, "I'm coming over," and I would practically click my heels in the air.

I climb into my Jeep (yes, I drive a Jeep, it goes great with the dress and the boots if that's what you are wondering), and I'm about to start the engine, and then, it really hits me. The Sadness.

His face appears before me so clearly he might as well be sitting right there — his dark, wide eyes gleaming like when he tells a joke. He's got this cute crooked smile that makes a dimple on one cheek. He's got great hands, buttery smooth, and strong.

Did he not see the magical things we were going to accomplish together? In our relationship? In our complementary careers? In the church? It felt like this was what God wanted too, not just me, or him.

And it turns out he had this whole other life — and now he's gone. I've lost him. In fact, I never had him in the first place. My makeup is a mess — I mean, I am balling like a cliché out of some rom-com. Except I already know it's not going to end in a wedding.

8:13 A.M.
My Jeep bounces along the boulevard just after I wipe down my face and reapply. Ugh, now I'm really disappointed in myself. There is no denying it — I got played, hustled, hoodwinked.

Predictably, Drake's "Best I Ever Had" song comes on the radio, and the memories flood back: At the concert, Charm looked so fine that night. I was so proud to be on his arm, while other unattached women looked him up and down. It was a warm night, and we danced the whole time.

For some reason, a story Charm told me pops into my head about his great uncle falling asleep during a wedding. "He snored so loud during the service, the pastor had to wake him up." I laughed so hard when he told me that story, I cried. Why that song sparked that memory, I have no idea.

Drake sings: *Baby, you my everything, you all I ever wanted*
We could do it real big, bigger than you ever done it…

"Nope!" I practically shout and snap the radio off. I do *not* need to redo my makeup for a third time today.

8:55 A.M.
I arrive at work. Immediately, I cross to the coffee station and grab a mug. I don't usually care for coffee, and I have never had a sip of alcohol in my life (with one horrible exception), but today, I'm going for the coffee. I hear someone behind me.

"What's up, girl?"

It's my co-worker, Jean. Although we don't have much in common, she has always been nice to me. She's also really good at her job. "Hey,

Jean," I paste a smile on my shiny lips. I just don't want to get into it. "Same-old Wednesday."

Jean acts surprised by everything, even when there's nothing to be surprised by. Jean tells me the latest work gossip with utter disbelief and then pauses.

"Are you okay? You seem, I dunno." Who am I kidding? The last few weeks I have really been miserable. There is no way my co-workers haven't caught on.

"Yeah, I'm okay, just didn't sleep great last night." I lie. Then say a two-second prayer asking for forgiveness. Jean nods sympathetically, and we head to our desks.

I wave to my boss, Shelley, across the big open floor plan and get to work. I have two appointments with families that want home loans and one senior who is moving money from an IRA to a CD. Piece of cake.

Maybe I wouldn't have gotten so wrapped up in Charm's game if I hadn't met him in church. That's my safe place, where people are supposed to be good to each other, right? It wasn't like I saw stars the first time I met him. Did I?

He was a baller, literally, with all the associated bling: tall, built, beautiful skin, the most charismatic smile you've ever seen. That old saying that goes, "If it looks too good to be true, it probably is?" Yeah, that was Charm.

Not long after our introduction, he took the next step and sent a Facebook request. Disclaimer: I know how social media makes everyone paranoid and distorts our connections.

I accepted the request; there was no harm in being friends, right? But when I would post something, he'd respond to it in a DM rather than a comment. I wouldn't have noticed once, but on three or four posts, he never liked, never commented, always wrote something complimentary in a private message. It felt a little strange, but at the time, it didn't occur to me that he didn't want anyone to see us communicating.

I did what many of us do when we get a message from someone who's attractive, and their social media profile lacks red flags like cosplay or Nazis. I responded and carried on a bit of small talk.

> Charm: How u been?
> Me: I'm good, just working, doing lots of writing for the church, and my own work
> Charm: That's right, you said you were a writer. What kind of stuff do you write?
> Me: Well, I just started this new piece...

It felt nice to have the attention of someone so...shiny. But it was clear he was building his case. I needed to run for the hills. *I mean, like, sprint.* I'd cut the conversation short. But every time we happened to be online, those little chats got longer.

Here's what you're going to do, I'd tell myself, *throw his arrogant, self-absorbed butt in the friend zone and hold the line. You can handle a friendship with an attractive guy. And don't judge a book by its cover. Keep conversation light, don't sleep with him and you should be fine.*

Oh Candace.

He came on strong, showering me, no, *drenching me* with compliments: "I love your style. It's really dope, like you would look good in anything."

"Do the men at your job stop talking when you walk in?"

"I don't know anyone who reads as much as you do."

Still, I held the line. And so I was unprepared for what happened next: We actually became cool. "Friends it is," he told me. And we kept talking. He didn't lose interest just because I resisted his advances. There he was, every Sunday, always the polite gentleman. One Sunday, he glided to the podium, which surprised me. He preached this great sermon, about seeing God in everyone around you, even if they don't see it in themselves. His reverberating voice filled the space. It was inspiring, and when he finished, I was breathless.

After the service, he came over and politely shook my hand, like he always did.

"That was a really powerful message, and I like what you said, about trying to find that reflection of God in everyone every day."

"I don't always succeed," he laughed, "but when I do, my interactions with people usually go a lot better." I couldn't help it — I was moved by all this.

He asked about me and listened like he cared about my answers. He even gave good advice. Eventually, the conversation became long enough to justify lunch.

One lunch turned into a few dinners. To make sure we were on the same page, I would slide in an "I met a guy," and "Do you think this is a nice first date outfit?"

Again, he surprised me. "Yes, in fact you make quite the first impression," he'd respond. Or "Tell me about him, is he worthy of you?"

Before I knew it, I was telling him EVERYTHING. Every crush, hope, dream, and he listened, remembered, made sure I looked on the bright side when I was feeling low.

"I watched too many Disney movies growing up. I *still* watch too many Disney movies," I confided to him. I guess this is as good a place as any to explain, Reader, that I was really obsessed with Disney.

"What's wrong with Disney movies?" he asked.

"Nothing, I have a huge weakness for them. I'm just starting to think that 'happily ever after' thing is make-believe."

"Now hold on," he cleared his throat like this was serious, "I mean, if you want some dude to, like, slay a dragon and ride a white horse through Detroit and carry you off to his castle, then yes, you're right. But true love? That's not make-believe."

"You think? Then why are all my friends married or in committed relationships, and I'm still single?"

"Well, you're picky."

"Wha?" He had me going.

"No, you should be. You aren't like any girl I've ever met before. Not just any guy can date someone like you. You're special."

"You're such a good friend," I would tell him, partly because I wanted to hold the line, but partly because it was true. I held that line so hard, I shook.

But having Charm in the friend zone was so, so nice! I had a guy's perspective, someone who'd grab a movie with me when I didn't have a date or my girls weren't available. He knew what I liked, and he celebrated my wins. This was every girl's dream. Because there was no kissing or touching, I was able to relax and be myself. I knew he was attracted, but he wasn't imposing his wants on me, and I was relieved.

And yet. My heart had other plans.

It would be late at night, we would both be lying in bed FaceTiming, and he'd ask, "So how did that date go? The one with the attorney?"

I'd say something like, "Oh, it was okay, I guess."

"You sound overwhelmed."

I'd laugh. "Yeah, I know. He's nice and all, and I think he really likes me. There's just something missing."

"That spark?"

"Yeah! You can't fake that, you know?"

"Oh, I know. It's either there, or it isn't." It was starting to become a problem that any other guy who came along couldn't measure up to Charm's banter. And so looking back, those other guys were no threat to him. They made him look great.

But he really took it up a notch when he started talking about his own romantic mishaps.

"She was the one everyone wanted, you know, and she knew it. I was with her for a few months, and I started to get the feeling that she really didn't care to get to know me, she just liked being seen with me."

"Oh, right. 'Ms. Look-at-Me.' "

"Yeah! I mean, I wasn't looking for something super serious, but she was posting all this stuff on Instagram, making us take selfies wherever we went, and like, when we were together, she didn't even seem interested. She never even asked me about my day."

"For real?"

"For real. I couldn't talk to her like we talk."

"Speaking of talking, it's 1 a.m.! I have to go."

"Time flies. Talk tomorrow?"

"You know we will."

"Goodnight, Beautiful."

Charm became the friend I never knew I needed, but never wanted to be without again. He could be arrogant, stubborn, sure, but he seemed to actually like it when I poked fun at him for it. And in the meantime, I was busy praising myself for handling this like an adult. *Candace, aren't you glad you didn't take off running?*

There was another thing at play here: I'm a late bloomer. I've only been in a couple serious relationships. I had some short-lived boyfriends, but very few relationships compared to Charm, and only one other long-term where talk of marriage appeared on the horizon. When all my girlfriends were meeting up with boys after school, I was at home, doing my homework, or vision boarding my future with pictures of the Eiffel Tower I cut out of my mom's old magazines.

In high school, I was super cautious, partly because of my protective family, partly because of my religion, and partly because I just couldn't be bothered with what passes for manners out there in the world. There was Nate. He is now married to a really nice lady, and they have twins. And then there was David, who was so square I would fall asleep in my chair when he talked.

So maybe things would have been different with Charm if I had a little more experience. I didn't have a lot of firsthand data to base my decisions on. Maybe I would have hit the eject button sooner had I dated a little more.

We would take walks sometimes, even in the winter in the frigid Michigan air, and I couldn't help but notice the way other women looked at him. They all looked: Half would shoot me a glance of admiration, the other half seemed to check to see if we were together.

He was gorgeous, not even up for debate. I couldn't exactly blame that other woman, Ms. Look-at-Me he told me about — it felt good to be seen with him.

He told me more stories about past relationships, where they went wrong. Usually he complained about the women, and sometimes I would push back. Instead of getting defensive, he would say something like, "Maybe you're right, I was far from perfect."

How was this guy single? I started to ask myself sitting across him at lunch or exchanging a glance at church. Dang, he looked good in that suit. And always with that perfect smile. In my most generous moments, I thought *sure, he's not perfect, but who is? This handsome, smart, sweet guy deserves love.*

The women he pursued obviously had issues. Deep rooted issues. Something must be wrong with them. They couldn't tell that the reason he was so nonchalant was because he had his heart broken before. I saw that too, that he was a bit arrogant in the beginning, but now that I knew him a little better, I'd say it was worth it to wait till that wall came down.

Rome wasn't built in one night! How come no one has any patience anymore? No time to connect, always judging each other in the blink of an eye.

Look Reader, I know you think I'm nuts. But I cared about Charm, enough to want him to be happy. There was only one logical thing to do after watching this pattern: Start giving him dating advice.

Again, the late-night FaceTime. "How was your date?" I asked, always partly hoping it didn't go well.

"Aw man. So bad. She got nasty with the waiter. You ever met someone who has all the right stuff: perfect eyes, perfect hair, perfect body —"

"Yeah okay I get it," I interjected.

"But like their attitude is so nasty that they just start to look ugly to you?"

"Oh yes, I know what you mean." Then I paused for effect and squinted into the screen like I was scrutinizing him. "But I wonder…"

"What?"

"These women you date all have similar issues. If it's a pattern, maybe you should look at that."

"Whadaya mean?"

I was lounging against my pillows. He was also in bed, wearing a soft, old T-shirt. Dear Lord, this man. "Well," I ventured, "you are attracting these women, and they fit all your outside criteria: They are beautiful, professional, ambitious, right?" Am I making an indirect play for myself here? We'll get to that later.

"Yeah, for the most part," he frowned a little, like he didn't see where I was going with this.

"But on the inside, they don't connect to you, and vice versa. So maybe you are choosing them because then you can do the rejecting. It stays on the surface because that's safe." I mean, why else did he have so many failed relationships?

His face clouded over.

"Candace," he said slowly. "Damn," he said more to himself. "You know what, you are right. Part of it is that I just have so much going on, with work and school and my fraternity. All the stuff I do for church." Business school hogged a ton of his time. It was challenging, and we talked about it a lot. He had dreams about becoming an entrepreneur. He was athletic, well spoken and a Christian. Did I mention all this?

"Uh huh." I nodded. And waited.

"But you're right, the women I date, a lot of them are…superficial."

"I wasn't going to use that word, but yeah."

"And, like, I have trouble opening up, so even when I am into someone, I act like I don't care. They think I'm selfish, inconsiderate, cocky. But I'm not, that's not really me. You are the first person to notice that." He did not miss the opportunity to bring the screen in close. He even looked right at the light of the camera so it appeared like he was making eye contact. Clever.

I had to resist the urge to put my hand over my heart since he could still see me. But it got to me. It really did.

I started actually getting angry at these women — why didn't they stick around long enough to see all the amazing things about him? What, they needed six figures and a fat rock on their finger within 90 days? *What's wrong with you, ladies!*

"You are a great guy, Charm. Don't worry, someday someone will see it."

He laughed, a sleepy, warm chuckle. "Oh you think so, huh?"

My now very close male friend and I had a bond that seemed as though it could never be broken. Days we didn't talk felt incomplete. During the friendship, we were in constant communication. Literally every day.

And then that night happened. The night I was practically in my pajamas when we saw a horror movie and ate Milk Duds. The night he broke the wall down. I don't even really remember the words he used, but his body language, his sincerity, the guts it took to say all that. It was the kind of thing women wait their whole lives for. I looked right past his horns, pitchfork and bright red skin, into his deep brown eyes and saw heaven.

5:18 P.M.

Wait, my shift is over? What did I even do today? I cannot go to Bible Study tonight. I feel horrible missing it, but if he was there, I'd have to leave, and if he wasn't there, I'd just be staring at his empty chair. Nope, going home.

6:34 P.M.

I push the door to my apartment open. My little dog Charlie is tap dancing in the hall, practically jumping up and down with his legs crossed like, "If you don't let me out right now, I'm going to go full racehorse on this floor!"

I keep my coat on, drop the takeout on the counter, and grab the leash. Oh, the relief on his little face!

It's already dark, and we circle the block slowly. I let him dawdle at each tree, and of course, I'm thinking about Charm. I still have that Drake song in my head from the morning. Charlie loved Charm too. He would even come out with me during the winter and stand in the freezing wind while Charlie did his business. When I would get frustrated with the occasional accident, Charm would clean it up, telling me, "He's just a puppy, don't be so hard on him." A puppy? He's four! It was so sweet. I'm not going to lie, I took this as a sign that Charm would one day be a patient daddy.

We head back home, Charlie now content with the world again after marking his territory about a half dozen times. I think about calling my mom, but I'm not quite ready for that yet.

Besides, he might call and we clear this whole thing up like it was just a big misunderstanding.

7:22 P.M.

Back at home, I unlock my front door and Charlie skitters across the floor. My takeout sits on the counter, but I'm not hungry.

I flop onto my couch with the TV on, but I'm scrolling through Charm's texts. And when I'm not doing that, I'm replaying our conversations in my head.

> Charm: You want me to be something I'm not...
> Me: Like honest, for example? Yeah, you're right

Or this one:

> Charm: You can be spoiled. You grew up with a silver spoon. You don't understand.
> Me: Neither do you. Obviously.
> Charlie: You should stop doing that to yourself.

I look up from my phone. Charlie is curled up on his little cushion on the ottoman.

"Did you say something?" I ask him out loud.

"Yeah, this is a waste of time. He was never right for you."

A huge sigh comes out of me. "Oh, Charlie."

"No really, hear me out. I mean, I liked the guy, Candace, he cleaned up my poops, and he knew about the spot to scratch behind the ear. But he had other stuff going on that you didn't know about. I could smell it on him."

"Wait, what? Why are you just now telling me this?"

Charlie's little eyebrows twitch like a tiny, wise old man. "Would you have believed me if I told you before?"

7:26 P.M.

My imaginary conversation with Charlie was cut short by my mom. She has a sixth sense for when I'm suffering. I get a text.

> Mom: Hellloooo??
> Me: Hi, Mom.
> Mom: Ah there you are. How are you, honey?
> Me: I'm good, just really busy at work. Lots of appointments.

I do not mention that I skipped Bible Study, and she doesn't notice. *Thank you, Jesus.* She would totally know something was up since I never miss a class.

> Mom: Well that's good, I'm glad to hear that. Call me tomorrow?
> Me: I will do my best, but don't be mad if I can't talk. By Friday, for sure.
> Mom: Okay, sweetheart. You sure you're okay?
> Me: 100 percent. Love you.
> Mom: Love you too.

7:36 P.M.

And right back to replaying conversations...

> Charm: We'd be better off as friends. *Translation: I need you psychologically, but I don't want the responsibility of being your boyfriend. In other words, I want to have sex with other people.*
> Me: Ok. *Translation: We WERE friends. You screwed it all up. Now you want me to accommodate your needs while*

you go hoeing around?

Charm: I still want to stay connected. *Translation: I just want to be able to reach out when it is convenient for me and count on you to carry my emotional baggage for me, is that cool?*

Me: Sure. *I'm too exhausted and confused to say anything else.*

I look over at Charlie expecting more opinions, but he has already fallen asleep.

8:29 P.M.

Maybe he'll realize he made a mistake.

I flash back again. Coming into work the day after we had "the talk" and more importantly, first kiss, I found a dazzling bouquet of roses greeting me at my desk. My co-workers gather around like excited puppies, practically pushing each other to get a view of the card.

"Oooooo! Candace had a hot date last night!" Shelley teased me. When I blushed everyone hooted and pointed at my face.

As I opened the card, my co-workers tried to contain themselves. "Well?" Jean finally piped up.

The card read:

> *Candace, this was the only way I knew how to express myself after last night. You are a truly amazing woman, and I'm so lucky that I know you.*
>
> *Your Man,*
Charm.

I finished reading it, and a stupid huge grin spread across my face. Jean and Shelley peered over the card, and I'm telling you, they practically howled. The general manager came out of his office upstairs and shook a finger at us. We laughed and went back to work. I stared at those roses all week. I read that card a million times.

And it wasn't once. I got those beautiful flowers many times. So many times, my co-workers would look over and yawn.

What would I do if he sent them now? He snaps out of it, realizes he can't live without me and he'll apologize and want to sort things out.

Where did we go wrong? He started accusing me of being selfish. I never, and I mean NEVER, took those gestures for granted. I mean, I am a bit spoiled…but he spoiled me, right? He set the bar, calling and texting multiple times a day, taking me to shows, making dinner reservations. When we first started dating, he lavished me with jewelry and surprise chocolates. I'm not going to lie, it felt nice — who doesn't love that? — but it was the connection, the sweet face of the guy I knew and meaningful conversation I fell in love with. Gifts and stuff are luxuries — they aren't necessary for 21st century dating, or my heart, for that matter. I'm down with Netflix and chill! And I understood he was busy.

I start wondering if I've been asking for too much? Was I being needy? I mean, conversation is not that important. Psh. Why would I need to talk to him? Dates, Smates! I don't need to go out. Those types of luxuries aren't necessary for 21st century dating. Do I really want to throw the entire year and a half away?

I wonder if I'm somehow to blame. Are his actions toward me a result of me? Maybe this is all my fault. After all, he dumped me. Maybe I'm the issue?

Deep Breaths. This is nuts. What I need to do is get myself together. This is him, not me. If anything, he needs to call me, and beg me to take him back, and hope I even consider the thought. I am not calling! I am *not* going to be the girl who got dumped and calls back first. *I am not thirsty.* He knows my number. And until he calls back, we will not speak.

I'm Dr. Jekyll and Mr. Hyde.

What if he doesn't even call? What if he's really done? What if… what if I'm doomed to be single foreveeeerrrr?! Oh my goodness! I can't breathe! Where are these tears coming from? He is such a jerk. He's not worth my tears. I wish my body would listen. Don't cry…don't cry! Too late.

10:01 P.M.

Charlie and I are cuddled on the couch watching "The Bachelor." What is wrong with these people? Do they have an ounce of self-respect?

Oh no, I lean closer to the screen. Low and behold, there I am, sitting in that row of women, all of us in evening dresses. And there is Charm sitting there in his designer suit, his teeth sparkling white like a shark. The other women give me the stink eye as Charm talks.

"Candace is definitely the smartest out of all of them," he begins. I can't help but bat my eyelashes at that compliment, but then he goes on. "But she's also the most entitled. She grew up in this privileged home, and so she expects to be treated a certain way."

I'm mortified. The other women are smirking. "Hey," I snap, "that's not fair. It's also not true!"

And now I'm yelling at the TV like an old man. "I am not some kind of gold digger! I have a solid job, I take care of myself, I always went Dutch on our vacations!"

The nerve.

11:39 P.M.

Sleep feels about as doable as deadlifting a full-grown man. I squirm around in my sheets, just can't get comfortable. The gears in my head are grinding: *I ask him why he canceled three dates in a row, and he fires back with, "I'm done?" Did I not have a legitimate reason to question him?*

If I had said it in another way, would that have changed the outcome of the conversation? I guess it doesn't really matter. That was history and so were we.

I sit up and whack my pillow. Charlie, whom I moved to his little bed in my room, whines and yawns, goes back to sleep. I'm jealous of Charlie.

To dump me on the day of Bible Study, that is just so cold.

This feels horrible. My heart is toast. I refuse to stay in this state of mind. I'm putting a cap on this whole breakup thing. I'm giving myself ten days to get over this. Seven days wouldn't quite be enough, and he sure doesn't deserve two weeks. That's it, ten days. In fact, I'm already counting today. Nine days from now, it will be like Charm never existed.

CHAPTER TWO

THURSDAY

7:16 A.M.

It is a grey day out there. I'm not getting out of bed today. I can't go on. This is the end. Hide my keys. Hide all sharp objects. Check my pulse. If you're wondering, day 2 sucks.

Okay, I do get up and instantly regret it. I got hit by a bus yesterday. Today, I feel the full impact, almost soreness, and heaviness. If you have ever been in an accident, you know that special "next day" pain.

Going to bed with no goodnight text was just as bad as waking up to no good morning text. Everything reminds me of him: love songs, floor tiles, bags of garbage, even the poop Charlie was kind enough to leave on my floor this morning. Thanks, pal. I can't even muster the words to chastise my dog. First Charm craps on me, and now the dog craps on my floor. It's Crap Day. I should call into work sick.

I squat down on the floor and clean up the mess while Charlie looks sheepish. It's not his fault. I should've taken him out one more time last night. "Sorry, Charlie. I promise I'll do better. You're all I have left. You're my longest relationship. You won't leave me will you, boy?"

"Where would I go? I'm not 'Born Free' over here."

"Aw, 'Born Free,' I love that movie. Let me just take care of your mess for you, and then we'll go for a walk. Would you like that?"

"You know I'd like that! Can I pee on some trees and smell some other dogs' butts?"

I click on his leash and we head out. A walk through the neighborhood sounds really good right now. Some fresh air, that's what I need. If I stay in the house, I'll think of him. And what he did to me. I'm not going to sit around and waste away while he's probably out living his life. Not thinking of me. He can't be, if he was he'd call. But he hasn't. Oh well. His loss.

The city is bustling, just like any Thursday. I walk by the corner store, wave hello to the guy stacking fruit. I should buy more fruit. Then I wave to the lady at the Chinese restaurant where I get my takeout. I should buy less takeout.

We get to the little park a few blocks away, where people are jogging, sitting on benches drinking coffee, taking their dogs out. "Well, I officially have 24 hours of being single under my belt. This feels worse than I thought it would. Not only did my one-and-a-half-year relationship end, but so did my two-year friendship. Why would he do this?"

Not only does Charlie not respond, but he shoots me a look like, "We are in public and you know I don't really talk because I'm a dog, right?" I look down and I'm still in my pajamas, with my coat and sneakers on. No wonder people are looking at me funny.

7:31 A.M.

That's it. I'm calling in, taking a Mental Health Day. I dial work and Shelley picks up.

"I'm sick," I tell her, and the thing is, this isn't exactly a lie. The last few weeks, with this tug-of-war with Charm, I have been so depleted that my co-workers have been giving me that "I am concerned" face. I stopped putting myself together, my light went out, I've been running on fumes. I actually touch my forehead as we talk to make sure I don't have a fever.

"Oh, poor you," Shelley says. "You just take care of yourself, Candace. I hope you feel better soon."

This is the wonderful thing about working at a bank: They take really good care of their employees. And their policies border on germaphobia.

"I will, thanks Shelley," I say in my most scratchy voice. Lord, forgive that little white lie. Seldom do I use my sick days, and I need some time to think. And cry.

We are back at my apartment. The mail is overflowing from my box. Probably nothing but bills. See, somebody's thinking about me! I'm going to need a second job if my expenses keep pouring in like this. That's an idea, a worthy distraction, maybe a little freelance writing work? A second job will bring in some extra money. Plus, it'll give me something to do. Plans!

I just need to stay busy. I can do that. I *need* to do that. After a little fresh air and an English muffin, I feel new determination. If it takes all the tissue and ice cream in the world, so be it, because I'm not going to call! I won't. I refuse to! As bad as I want to, and I really, really want to.

I start imagining a TV game show called "Where's My Dignity?" and as a contestant, I bravely fight off the temptation to call my now ex-boyfriend:

Game show host: Candace, for the grand prize of $1 million, will you call Charm?

Me: I refuse. (audience applauds)

Dignity, who made up that word? How is it undignified to call him? I wonder if I would lose my dignity if I text him. I can hear the dignity police filling out their report.

Dignity Officer 1 (looking down at a chalk outline on my apartment floor): It looks like she put up a struggle, she resisted calling, but then she finally gave in and texted. So tragic.

Dignity Officer 2: What a shame, if only she could have held out a few more days, she wouldn't have completely destroyed her dignity.

8:17 A.M.
"I'm single." This is my first time saying it out loud. Oh, I don't like how it sounds. Not one bit. Who made up that word anyway, "single?" I'm not a slice of Velveeta, or a scoop of ice cream. When did we start referring to unmarried, uncoupled people as "single?"

I'll tell you who made up that word: The same person who made up the word "dignity," that's who! Somebody who recently got married or is in a relationship and wanted to distinguish herself from her friends. I can hear her now while she peruses her wedding photos:

"Don't you worry just because you are…umm…umm…single! That's what you are — single because you are not part of a team. We are on Team Us, and you are on Team You! Really, I'm sort of jealous of you. I mean, not really, but think of all the stuff you can do *by yourself* because YOU ARE ALONE! You can see whatever movie you want, you can always pick the restaurant and you have your entire bed to yourself."

The married woman who invented those terms should be slapped. On a Wednesday, of course.

As I get older (and I'm not *that* old, only 29), I notice that after my friends get married, they call less, we hang out less and when photos of them pop up on Facebook, they are vacationing and socializing with other married people. And once they have kids, forget it. They might as well be ghosts. I'm pledging now not to do that to my unmarried friends. That is, if I don't stay "single." ARGH!

You know what will now be more painful than a root canal? Weddings! Before Charm and I started dating, when we were just friends according to the verbal contract, one of his guy friends from business school got married. He asked me if I wanted to be his "date." I joked about being his surrogate girlfriend and that his guy friends would mistake me for the real thing.

"That's my whole game," he laughed, "let them think that." It was a crazy wedding with a full band, a big train on the dress, a cake several stories tall. All the things. The DJ played good music, and while Charm had quite a few, and his buddies had quite a few more, we had a really good time on the dance floor. His friends all night kept coming up to us and saying drunkenly, "Now who is this, Charm? You didn't tell us about *her*." There is something about weddings where the attendees all hope that the romance magic is going to sprinkle down on every other not-yet-married couple in the room. That was certainly the case with Charm. We went to three weddings in the time we were dating, and everyone always asked us, "So, are you next?" One time, my girlfriend positioned me right behind her when she went to toss the bouquet. Of course, I didn't catch it. My other friend caught it, and guess what? She's married now.

Still, going to weddings with Charm was so much better than going alone.

Right before I met him, my friend, let's call her Selfie, enlisted me to be her de-facto wedding planner. Her guy, Mr. Selfie, was the son of one of my mom's friends, a schoolteacher and a really nice guy. I introduced Mr. Selfie to Mrs. Selfie, and so somehow, I was pressured into doing all kinds of organizing for her. Now I knew it was her special day, and on your special day, you tend to get a little narrow in your thinking, but Mrs. Selfie was off the chain with bossing everyone around. That meant me and her mom, everyone.

Finally, I had to say to her, "Look, I love you, but you need to stop biting everyone's head off."

She looked at me like I just slapped all that expensive makeup off her face. Her mama even said, "Candace is right, honey. Everything is going to be fine."

She went postal. I mean atom bomb. "What do you mean, this is MY WEDDING. I get to do this ONCE, and who are you to tell me..." Bridezilla. I have seen this so many times. What is it about getting married that makes people completely lose their mind? She spun her wheels for a little longer then burned off all that anxiety and finally calmed down.

I couldn't help but notice I didn't get a thank you card, not even after all that running around I did! Now, Mr. And Mrs. Selfie have a bunch of mini-selfies running around on their rug. I don't see them much at all either.

And I'm alone. There's that word again, alone. I'm back BY MYSELF. I look at my phone. My brain is fighting the whole idea that he just checked out on our whole enterprise. As I wander around my cute little apartment, now piling up with takeout containers and Ben & Jerry's cartons, I'm wracking my brain to figure out if there was something I could have done differently. Was I being unreasonable when he suddenly disappeared off the mat? No. Was I being "paranoid" when I didn't just go along with his program and pretend like it didn't hurt? No.

My pacing around isn't helping. I'm looking for something that isn't there.

8:32 A.M.

Who am I kidding. My cute little apartment is a complete mess. I worked hard to get this place to my taste, and I take pride in keeping it organized and clean. Right now, it looks like a bulldozer tore through it.

I'm still in my pajamas. Seriously? This is only DAY TWO?

Then something else occurs to me. What if I am missing something. What if all that stuff that was "not my business" was real trouble, and he just wasn't telling me? It's not like him to not confide in me, but what if someone got hurt, someone is dying, some family member did something embarrassing? Or worse, what if something bad happened to Charm, and he doesn't want me to know so he's hiding it? What if I am being horrible right now, just defending my own ego, when he's in danger? Just because we are not in a *relationship* doesn't mean I stop caring about him as a person.

I sit down at my laptop. Yep, you guessed it. I ditched the Dignity Police long enough to snoop on him on social media. Not to my surprise, he's alive. I'm a little relieved but also disappointed there isn't another explanation aside from "he's a total jerk." He has posted three times within the last 24 hours. He shared some dumb meme, but he also posted a pic with a bunch of guys out drinking beer at some sports bar. Well, it took less than 24 hours for him to completely move on. Is there some law that says men have to go out and get wasted with their boys whenever they go through a breakup?

Suddenly I notice I can't breathe. My stomach hurts. My eyes burn. It's over. It's really over. I wasn't going to say anything until I knew for sure. It's been 24 hours, and I still haven't heard from him. I can't believe this. It's really over. I'm about to pass out. I need to go to the emergency. *Candace, calm down!*

9:40 A.M.

My phone rings. I must still be holding out hope, because every time my phone goes off, I run to it half expecting it to be him. Instead, it's my girlfriend, "Dreamer," and I've been dodging her for days.

I don't feel like talking. But what else am I going to do? Clean? Pay bills? Yeah right.

Let me pull myself together enough to talk to my girl. She may be going through something too that she needs her friend for. *Try not to be so self-centered*, I tell myself. And yet, I'm dreading this conversation because I know what she is going to say.

"Hey Dreamer."

"Hey Girl! Where you been?"

Dreamer runs her own consulting firm, and so she can call me anytime she likes. I can practically see her tiny frame seated at her desk, her perfect short, sassy hair, her nails a shiny bright pink.

I tell her what happened with Charm and instantly regret it.

"You need to apologize!" is the first thing out of her mouth.

"I need to do what?!"

"He is out there working hard to make something of himself. He's your 'Happily Ever After!'"

"No, he isn't, and he doesn't want to be, that's my point. I've been through this with him so many times."

"Call him back!" yells Dreamer, who is happily married to the sweetest guy in the world. Sometimes I feel like she still believes in fairy tales. Let me be clear. She did not invent the word "single" or "dignity," and she has been loyal to me. That said, she has always championed Charm as my future husband, and sometimes, her vision on this is, well, skewed.

It's crazy after all Charm put me through that she still thinks I'm wrong. I can still hear her voice ringing in my head: "Okay? Why would you say 'okay' when he asked you if you just wanted to be friends? Especially when you weren't 'okay' with what he said! You should fight for your relationship. He's scared, Candace. And building a foundation takes time." Girl missed her calling. She should have been an attorney because, boy can she pick apart an argument.

The truth about Dreamer is, she always sees the good in people. I met Dreamer in sixth grade on the first day of school. She's the girl who's pretty but will never admit it. She dropped out of college to take a leap of faith and start her own consulting business. She's now one of the top ten consultants in our area. She married her high school sweetheart, Mr. Dreamer (but not before a long, dramatic breakup and reunion). She's active in her church and still finds time to volunteer. Dreamer is the type of girl who has accomplished most of her dreams, and in her world, if you don't have the husband, the job, or the life you want, you're doing something wrong. Not that her life is perfect, but when she wants something, she just goes out and gets it.

She hasn't always been in love with love. Dreamer became a "love expert" after she reconciled with Mr. Dreamer who cheated on her and got another girl in our class pregnant. I know, it was truly horrible. It was high school, what can I say. When she discovered this, I had to hold Dreamer back from tearing his face off.

But then he surprised all of us by really working hard to win her trust back. After ten years of dedication, he finally restored Dreamer's faith in him. She even has a relationship with Mr. Dreamer's son, which blows my mind. They're the couple that gives the scripture "love never fails" meaning.

So this is a totally risky phone call because I almost believe her, and when I get off the call, I'm more tempted than ever to dial Charm's number. I look at the screen with my finger on the button.

"No," I say out loud and put down the phone. Almost! Dreamer's romantic notions are screwing with my real life. She's not right about this. Our breakup is not my fault.

She might be right that he is going through a lot at the moment. But that doesn't justify any of this.

I need a reality check. I need to talk to "Stay Woke."

11:11 A.M.
"Oh hell no."

Thank God for my girl, Stay Woke. She does it for me all the time! We all need someone like this in our lives — someone who keeps it real and tells you how it is, even if that means the occasional gut check. Every woman needs friendships with balance. Dreamer inspires hope, but Stay Woke is going to save me from calling Charm and apologizing to him for breaking my heart.

Stay Woke is a curvy, dark-skinned beauty with natural hair, a flawless smile and fondness for bright colors. She's older than Dreamer and me, just not sure by how much. I met Stay Woke about ten years ago when we both worked at a restaurant and bonded over how much we hated waiting tables. It didn't take us long to discover how much we had in common. And we've been inseparable ever since. I've seen her through a failed marriage, single parenthood and her ownership of the restaurant we both hated waitressing at so much. It's a great place to eat now, by the way. She's also the best boss.

Stay Woke has accumulated multiple businesses; she even has her own travel agency. I love her for her zero-BS policy when it comes to love and relationships. She has the same mindset with love that she does with business: If you don't want to be here, don't let the door hit you where the good lord split you.

It's probably not an accident that the people I love and admire have this entrepreneurial streak. I gravitate to people who break out and do their own thing. I wish I had a thing. But writing? For a living? I'd still be paying my college debt in my 70s!

Anyway, back to Stay Woke. This conversation will be tricky for a totally different reason. The tough part about this situation with Charm is she never liked him, and she was always trying to get me to kick him to the curb. He was too inconsistent, too controlling, too good-looking, even. It put me in a position of having to defend him. Will she say something harsh like, "I warned you?"

"Yeah," I cringed, bracing for her reaction. "He dumped me in a text. I guess that's better than a Post-it."

"You took the day off work?"

"Yeah, I'm a mess." And I go into it. Again. Not like she hasn't heard it. But this is why we love our friends, right? Because they listen to us. Even when we are spinning like a broken record. As I'm talking, I can hear her mind working. She was right about a lot of the things she said. But, of course, she says the thing I need to hear.

"I'm sorry, girl. I know how disappointing all this is. And on the day of Bible Study? That's just cold. I hate to say it, but you know I am not surprised. This is his pattern."

"I know."

"He wanted to have his cake and eat it too. So you do some grieving, some praying, some retail therapy. God has something better in store for you." I hope she is right.

"You know what you should do?"

"What?"

"How about Fiji? It's not monsoon season."

"Come again?" I look at my phone like I heard her wrong.

"Sorry, Candace, I was talking to Carrie, my assistant. Anyway, as I was saying, you should call that guy you met at Starbucks."

"Oh, I don't know about that."

"Ye-ah!" She draws the "e" out for emphasis. I can hear her typing in the background. I guess it's too big a task to have undivided attention at 11:00 a.m. on a Thursday. "What? Thank you. Now where were we? Candace, you need to get your mind off that grown boy."

"Dreamer thinks I should call him back and apologize."

"Hold on now, what? I repeat: No. Hell no. You didn't do anything wrong! That's called accountability!" Stay Woke is big on accountability. "That's all on him. He had nothing to bring to the table. Not a chair, not a plate, not a napkin, not a damn thing! That's on him."

She's right about Charm. It's a relief to hear someone I trust say it, even if she has said it before. Stay Woke assures me we will continue the conversation. I thank her for not rubbing it in and hang up.

12:31 P.M.

The time has been going so slow. It's like I don't have anything to look forward to. I'm still camped out on my couch, eating grapes and popcorn, watching HGTV.

Sometimes my friends feel like the angel and the devil on my shoulders, but they can change roles and confuse me. Right now, Dreamer feels like the sassy little demon sitting on my left shoulder whispering, "Call him," while Stay Woke is a plump little angel whispering, "Walk away, you are better than this."

Stay Woke is right, in this case, and here is the main evidence in her argument: He didn't do this when we were just friends. During the friendship, we were in constant communication. And then after that fateful night when he made his case, everything started to change. Once we started dating, he would fall off, no explanation. He drank, which at first was fine with me, but sometimes, his behavior would change. He would become testy, or even judgmental. It was clear sometimes he was hungover, and that worried me. But the thing that made Stay Woke really sound the alarm was the vacation argument.

1:43 P.M.

As I mentioned, ever since I was a child, I was quite obsessed with Disney movies. *"The Little Mermaid," "Cinderella,"* even *"Lady and the*

Tramp." Come on, that scene where the dogs eat spaghetti isn't romantic? Then you have no heart whatsoever!

Anyway, part of my Disney dream involved the romance capital of the world: Paris. I always imagined my true love would either propose to me in front of the tower or take me there on my honeymoon. I have yet to visit Europe, nor do I speak a lick of French, but I have always longed to go there. With my happily ever after.

Oh, excuse me for a moment. I just need to blow my nose. Okay, that's better.

A few months ago, right before things went completely south, Charm and I started planning our next vacation.

"Mexico?" I asked him. We were cuddled up, lounging on my couch after dinner.

"I went last year for spring break. It was kind of crazy. I mean, it's nice there, but there is the tourist thing, and then there are some really bad neighborhoods. Like, you don't want to go down the wrong street."

"Ok, no," I said, scrolling down a page I found of top vacation spots on my phone. "What about Montreal?"

"Too cold." He yawned. Then he said casually, "Why don't we go to Paris?" I remember looking up, our eyes meeting, a long silence passing between the two of us.

"Paris?" I think I squeaked when I said it. He was smiling at me, a big, devious grin. "You know that is my dream, right?"

"Well, then, Candace Parker, I'm about to make your dream come true." He kissed me, and I shivered.

The next day I got on the phone with Stay Woke.

"I need you to book me some airline tickets." I told her, holding myself back as best I could.

"Oh yeah, where you going?" I could tell she was barely listening to me, so I waited.

"Charm asked me to go to Paris with him."

A pause. "Paris?" She asked, as if she heard me wrong. "Are you getting married?"

"Oh no, no," I rushed in, but in the back of my mind I was thinking, maybe?

"I thought you always said you were going to wait to visit Paris for your honeymoon?" She was testing me, trying to poke holes in my plan. Or make sure I wasn't hiding any crucial piece of information.

"Well, I'm in love, that counts as a good enough reason to go," I defended. I knew she wasn't going to be happy for me. As I have pointed out, Stay Woke's opinion of Charm is pretty low to the ground. She even told me once that he doesn't blink enough. Or maybe too much. Or not the right way. I forget.

"Well, okay, if you are sure, when do you want to go?" And then we started the process of reservations. We did this way in advance, and paid off the trip slowly so that we wouldn't go into debt. One of the advantages of having a travel agent as a best friend.

"So you have to pay these tickets off in five months." She still sounded skeptical, but I ignored her.

"Thanks, Stay Woke."

"And he better grow up and put a ring on your finger," she said, before hanging up.

2:47 P.M.

I just took a nap. Watched *"Pretty Woman."* Now, I'm watching *"Alien."* Somehow, it feels really good to watch Sigourney Weaver kill those little vicious, self-serving bastards. Wonder what that's all about.

6:02 P.M.

The sunset is beautiful today. My apartment has this little peek-a-boo view of the skyline. The colors change so slowly, it's hard to tell they are changing at all until it starts to get dark.

Tried to journal, tried to eat, tried to exercise. Nope. Just watched the clouds go by. I must stink.

"You know you stink," Charlie says. He's right. I go into the bathroom and fill the tub. Apparently, I'm out of bubble bath, but I find some salts and light a few candles.

I put my hair up and climb into the water. It's so hot, it's going to cook all the sadness right out of me. If only it was that easy.

8:54 P.M.

Oh crap. I sit back in my chair. Did I just spend almost two hours on social media looking for clues? Ouch, my back! Blinking is difficult, and my eyes have filmed over. And what did I learn? Nothing.

What mystery am I trying to solve that I don't already know the answer to? When I get up, my legs wobble like there's no blood in them. I barely brush my teeth and stumble into bed. But at least I think I can get some sleep. Zzzzz.

CHAPTER THREE

FRIDAY

This day is just…gone. I don't remember anything. Even if you hypnotized me, I could not recall a single detail of this day.

CHAPTER FOUR

SATURDAY

8:10 A.M.

My alarm goes off. My eyelids feel heavy, even though I slept eleven hours.

It's day 4, and I feel absolutely NOTHING. I'm not happy, I'm not sad. I don't feel up, I don't feel down. I'm not emotional, I'm not even angry. I just don't feel a thing. Numb is fine, numb is doable. It's so much better than the last three days.

I have a meeting at church, but I don't feel like going. I know it's not God's fault, or my ministries fault I'm in this mess. But I don't feel like fake smiling and saying, "I'm okay," for the millionth time when someone asks, "How are you?" I just don't want to.

Feelings, what are those? And why do they continue to get me in so much trouble? One day you're on my side, and the next day you're nowhere to be found. You're really loud at times, running the whole show, but on days like this, you say nothing at all, not even a whisper.

Alright Candace, enough moping. Get it together, girl. People are counting on you.

As I brush my teeth, a memory comes back. When we went to the Bahamas. It was my idea to book trips way in advance, and then pay them off slowly before the travel date. The businessman in him loved this, and so it became part of our courtship to daydream about where we would go next.

I spit in the sink and wipe my face.

We were in bathing suits, lounging on a white beach, the blue of the ocean is the bluest thing I had ever seen. Charm was wearing a white short-sleeve shirt with only a few buttons holding it closed as the breeze ruffled his collar. His skin was so gorgeous in the sun under that white shirt. He took a sip of his drink and smiled before he gave my hand a squeeze.

"It doesn't get much better than this."

"No," I told him, leaning back in my deck chair and closing my eyes. "It doesn't get much better than this."

I'm leaning on my sink, can't even look at my face in the mirror.

10:00 A.M.

The conference room is a no-frills space off the main church. Our congregation is non-denominational, about 400 members, and a lot of smiling faces. As usual, there are snacks, and I wouldn't normally indulge, but someone brought brownies and I didn't eat breakfast. This might be the only meal I eat today. Dang, that is really good. So at least my taste buds have not gone the way of the dodo like my feelings.

"Candace!" There is a team of about six ladies and seven men that I usually work with, and they all come up and hug me one at a time, give me a squeeze, and say something warm like, "Glad you are here," without asking a word about Charm.

I can't tell if they know or not — word travels fast around this campfire — but I decide it doesn't matter. Not today. I'm here to do the work, not think about myself, or my breakup, or my future. We go over what projects everyone is working on and their progress.

There is always so much to do. My church takes community organizing seriously so there is always a drive or an event or something that requires organization and teamwork. Usually, I would do more, but today, I measure out my energy a little more carefully. I take on a few pieces of copy for fliers I know I can deliver easily. It will feel good to write. We have a few laughs and then we pray together and wrap up.

I can't believe I was almost going to miss this meeting. I'm so glad I went. Focusing on something bigger than me gave me perspective. This was why social work appealed to me — it gave me a way to help others. I should bake some cookies next time.

11:07 a.m.
I left my phone in the car so I wouldn't keep looking at it every five minutes. Still not one call from you-know-who, but now I've got an email from a publisher. It must be bad news. Of course it's bad news. I can't open it, not today, I just can't. I'm not equipped to handle the effects of this breakup along with the aftermath of another rejection letter. Nope, this email will have to wait. Then a text comes in.

    Mr. Starbucks: Hey Stranger

No way. Stay Woke just mentioned him, wasn't that yesterday? Good grief, time sure moves slowly when you break up with someone.

This is the guy I was dating for a minute right before Charm and I became a thing.

Alright, I know what you are going to say, that all my other suitors paled in comparison, but it just so happens that I was really interested in this guy who sidled up to me in a Starbucks and started a conversation. That's the moment Charm chose to go in for the kill. And I stopped answering Starbucks's texts.

He's tall, a conservative dresser, played college basketball at Michigan State (I guess I have a thing for ballers), drives a beemer and is obviously into me.

I call him back. "Hey there, it's been a minute? How's everything with you?"

"I'm straight, you know, working hard, playing hard. I was just thinking about you, wondering how you been."

"Aw, that is so sweet. I was actually just thinking about you too."

What, it's true! I mean, not the way I said it, exactly.

After 20 minutes of catching up, he asked if I wanted to meet up with him for dinner tomorrow.

"I was thinking Vicente's, you know that Cuban place downtown? It's really good. And they have a live band."

A change of scenery sounds perfect. "Sounds like a plan! Can't wait to catch up."

"Me too, Candace. It's been too long. I'll pick you up at 7:00?"

"Alright, I'll see you tomorrow."

12:19 P.M.

Well, how about that? One door closes, and another opens and takes you to dinner. I group text Dreamer and Stay Woke.

> Stay Woke: Good for you, get out there and live it up. Have fun, Girl.
> Dreamer: So that's it, two days and you're already ready to move on? Candace, don't give up on Charm. I'm telling you, he's probably at home miserable because he let you go.
> Stay Woke: Well if that is true, then he has himself to blame.

I'm strolling with Charlie, reading my messages, and this time, Dreamer is the dainty angel on my shoulder, while Stay Woke is the evil spirit trying to tempt me.

> Dreamer: He's going to call, and you're going to kick yourself for even being in contact with Starbucks.
> Stay Woke: Oh no you don't sit around waiting for that fool to call you.
> Dreamer: Stay Woke, you are so cynical.
> Me: Uh...

I can practically feel their little speech bubbles punching me on one cheek and then the other as I walk down the street.

> Dreamer: Poor Starbucks, have you thought about how's he going to feel at the end of this? You don't even like him, you're just using him.

Okay, that's a good point.

> Stay Woke: It's just dinner! He's not offering to buy her a yacht! What's that thing you keep saying, "All you need is 10 days!" Shoot, with Mr. Starbucks you might be able to do it in 5. I approve of this message!

Also, another excellent point.

I understand where they're both coming from, but Stay Woke is right: I need to see if Charm managed to hypnotize me away from a potential connection, or if I was right and there was no "spark" between Starbucks and me.

I put my phone in my pocket but can still hear the two of them. Those two never agree on anything. But in the most loving way possible.

Besides, I have to get back into the swing of things, move on with my life. Sorry Dreamer, I can't agree with you on this one. This feels like a sign, and I'm going to make the most of it.

2:13 P.M.

But first, some retail therapy. Within a minute, my Jeep is bounding over the highway toward the mall. Just a few things, you know, what the magazines call "healthy self-care."

Moments later, I dashed through Somerset Mall. This moisturizer is expensive, but I really need to put something expensive on my face right now, and oh this bag! How cute is this? These strappy heels are perfect (I'm 5'7, no need to go nuts), and this flowy skirt. I am about to leave the mall when I walk by a window and stop. Okay, can I call this a sign? Because there is a dress in the display window that's black with a big, bright tropical flower across the front. Bingo! I hit the jackpot for my date with what's his name, I mean Starbucks, at Vicente's.

I go in, try it on, and not to be vain but let me be vain — it looks ideal, rides my curves, even matches my glasses. Done and done! Alright, time to head home.

4:23 P.M.

Home. I drop my bags on my bed. Take a minute to sit on the couch, drink some water. If Charm cared about being friends the way he said he did, he would have called by now. I check my phone again. Nothing. All the sudden, I need to lie down in my bed. I push the shopping onto the floor. I'll clean the house tomorrow. In the evening.

What am I doing? Part of me wants to cancel this date. But I bought that dress, now I have to go. Again, I'm on that roller coaster. The enjoyment of waiting in line and anticipating the ride is exhilarating, but once I'm strapped in, the instant wave of terror overtakes me.

I proceed to go on because I have even proclaimed to my friends that I can handle it. I can't be the girl who has to take the walk of shame back through the line because she got scared. So, reluctantly, I stay. The ride begins, and it's filled with twists, turns, loops and drops at record speeds.

6:11 P.M.
Just woke up from a nap. Feeling drained. Drank some tea and now I'm trying to clean the house. This is what I refer to as my workout/cleanup combo. Charlie watches me with amusement while I put on an exercise video and pile everything on the sofa so I can vacuum. 1-2-1-2 with the right arm, 1-2-1-2 with the left arm. You know you can actually get your exercise and clean at the same time if you have a really terrible vacuum? Stop and do some jumping jacks, some squats. Back to vacuuming. Phew.

8:12 P.M.
Okay, so that lasted about ten minutes before I abandoned my cleaning efforts. This is something for which I can forgive myself. "Move it along," was my mom's philosophy, meaning, "hold the chaos at bay, even if you can't get it perfect." It's worth noting that the upper level of our house was always spotless, but the basement, which housed my mom's art supplies, was a disaster.

Growing up, I always kept my little corner of the bedroom neat and organized. This apartment is my safe place, and I'm always looking for little ways to improve it.

The look on my mom's face when I picked out the most simple, light grey modern sofa with a white end table for my apartment — I could not help but laugh at her horror.

"Give me a chance, Mom, this is just the beginning."

"Just don't forget: You are my daughter." She made a mock weepy face, and we laughed together.

Later on that day, I purchased teal and lavender vases, a large teal shag rug and a beautiful antique mirror. I found silk throw pillows in that blue-green neighborhood, and as soon as I put them on the couch, my mom sighed. But there was something missing.

My mom snapped her fingers. "Oh come on, how did I not think of this before? The paisley chaise lounge!"

It sounds awful, but hold on. The living room is a subtle combination of all those jewel peacock tones, with a little light green and dark cold purple, and it's perfect. The chest is light oak, and not at all yellow. And to think she found that thing at a yard sale on its way to the dump when she offered the guy twenty bucks!

Anyway, my apartment is what you might call "fully realized," and Charm used to compliment me on my attention to detail. He was quite handy, helping me put up shelves and rearrange furniture. We used to work so well together in the church. Whenever there was a function and they needed decorations or help setting up, Charm and I were the dream team. People in the congregation were always commenting about us. It felt so nice to have someone in my life who enjoyed my style, and it felt like we were practicing for the real thing.

I have so little energy, what is wrong with me? Maybe it's not just a broken heart. Maybe it's also blood sugar. I open the fridge. Oh my. There may as well be cobwebs in there. I sigh and shut the fridge. I find a can of soup, heat it up, drink it out of a mug. What am I now, some kind of cave man?

I turn on the TV and decide to do my nails.

CHAPTER FIVE

SUNDAY

9:02 A.M.

Church. I've been dreading this since Wednesday. Hmph, Wednesday. Just like with Bible Study, the anxiety of not knowing whether or not he'll be there is making me sick to my stomach. I get out of bed, do some stretches, walk and feed Charlie, then stand in front of the closet for nearly an hour agonizing over what to wear. What says, "Too Bad," and "Look What You Missed?" Polka dots? Gold Lamé? Snake skin?

What if he *is* there? What if he has the nerve to bring one of those women from the pictures to our church? He wouldn't do that, would he?

Oh great, now I'm seeing the front doors to the church open, and there is Charm, standing there in a tuxedo, with a little black box in his hand.

"Will you marry me?" he says, emotional, while he cracks open the little box and a diamond the size of my molar twinkles at me. I gasp.

"Oh Charm, I will! I will marry you!" I shout with all my heart.

And then I realize he's looking right past me, and there is the woman in the photo from the too-early-in-the-morning coffee date, Ms.

Look-at-Me, in a big puffy wedding dress. She puts her hand on her hip and raises her eyebrow at me.

So much for Paris.

Mauve blouse, new black skirt, heels. Done. Big sigh.

10:53 A.M.

It's a beautiful day as I set out for service. Big white clouds in a blue sky, that chilly early spring still keeping us on our toes. The Detroit skyline peers back at me on my drive to service. I'm nervous he might be there, but my instincts tell me he probably won't be.

Folks start to gather outside as I pull in and park. Our church is predominantly African American, but we have some other people of color and some white folks too. It's one of the things I like about this church, that it's so welcoming. It's also a beautiful old building that has been lovingly restored recently. The modern interior and small cafe makes for a great social area before and after service. The large screens in the halls begin to count down, indicating the service will soon begin. I almost made it to the sanctuary door before Alexis and her welcoming teams stops me.

I give hugs and shake hands while one eye surfs the crowd looking for him.

He's not here. Thank God. Really. Thank you.

We enter and the true majesty of the space immediately sets me at ease. Colored light streams in through the stained glass, and velvet, movie-style seats are a welcome change from hard wooden pews. Still more friendly faces file past and hug me, offering blessings, and kind words. No one says anything about Charm.

I sit down, relieved he's not here. I feel being here when he is not is life-saving. The music starts, and I close my eyes. We have a boisterous band and a choir of talented, hardworking singers who burst into big, beautiful song. The anointing is heavy. You don't know whether to sway, clap or cry. Everyone is dressed appropriately. However, there are a select few who live for attention, and the glitzy bold prints and big hats. Some men are in suits, which I find comforting: There is something special about a man in a suit. I like it when men take the time to dress up for church. I guess I don't have to repeat how good Charm looked in a suit.

"Break every chain, break every chain." I look around and see so many pleasant, happy faces, all glorifying God.

Service starts at 11:00 a.m. sharp, and every week the pastor stands before the congregation and begins with, "I won't be before you long." That always makes some of us chuckle and exchange looks because it's a lie — the pastor is always before us long. Today, he talks about self-worth, and how we may doubt ourselves, but Jesus never doubts us. "We are all worthy of love," he intones in his grandest voice. "Because we are all God's children." Amen.

The choir starts up again — they belt out notes straight from heaven. I close my eyes and take deep breaths as though I can inhale the sound itself. Waves of calm flow over me, and while the sharp edge of losing my man is there, this moment of prayer is a sweet relief. Thank you, God. Thank you.

1:22 P.M.

I'm back at home and something must be done about this apartment, for real this time. Look at this mess! I have been failing the Martha Stewart test all week. No wonder I am single, who would want to live like this? Just kidding. Sort of.

This time, I take out the duster as well as the vacuum; I roll up the carpets and put a CrossFit DVD on. I do jumping jacks in between opening the mail and mopping the kitchen. The laundry situation is crisis-level, so I attack that too. Fold everything, straighten everything. I even clean the window. Better! I need a break.

5:47 P.M.
It's getting close to my date. After I shower and wash all that house ick off me, I whip out the new dress and lay it on the bed. It's perfect for dancing and Cuban food! Black with a bird of paradise on the front and a cute frill at the bottom. I turn on the radio loud and dance in the bathroom as I do my hair and makeup.

I can do this! I'm single! I can date! And men want to date me! I pull on the dress and oh yes. I mean, it fits correct. I find my red stilettos and take a second look at my red lip. I start feeling like myself when Beyoncé comes on.

And now I'm in the humid crowd. It's late summer, and there she is on stage, singing her heart out. Charm is next to me, as we're pressed together, swaying to the music. He's got my hand against his warm chest, and he's smiling like he's never been happier in his life.

I sit down on the bed. Suddenly, I don't feel like dancing anymore.

6:58 P.M.
Right on time, the gold BMW pulls up in front of my apartment. I run down the steps, and he's on the sidewalk, holding the door open for me.

"Well good evening, Beautiful Lady." Starbucks is dressed in a polo shirt that looks more appropriate for a cruise. Or golf.

"Well, hello, sir."

"You are looking fine this evening."

"You're not so bad yourself." He closes the door after I slide in, and in a moment, we are on our way.

"It's so nice to see you again," he smiles at me eagerly. He's balding, a little, not that I mind that.

"Well thank you for the invitation."

The car glides along the overpass, revealing the dazzling lights of downtown Detroit. The night feels full of possibilities.

We arrive at Vicente's, and Starbucks pulls up to the valet who opens the door for me. Starbucks comes around and meets me at the ornate fountain in front. I take his arm, and we saunter in.

It was like we had just stepped off a plane and landed in Cuba. The sweet smell of plantains and spices washes over us, and the music grows louder as we enter the main room. The waiters dash around with plates of sizzling meats, beans, rice and crocks of soup.

A live band plays sultry Cuban music, while a few couples cut it up on the dance floor.

We arrive at our table, and Starbucks orders a mojito for himself and a faux-jito for me. Our drinks come with tiny umbrellas — some things never change.

"You look stunning tonight," Starbucks leans in.

"Thank you," I smile, but I have to look away from the force of his gaze. During our conversation, the sound of the band echoes off the colorful walls. He tells me about his work, his house, asks me about work and writing.

Then he says to me out of the blue, "Come on, let's dance!" He gets up and shimmies, kind of like your dorky uncle would at a wedding. Not the one that hits on you, the other one. You are so sweet, but also, could you stop?

He seems unaware that his moves are awkward, but he's gone to all this trouble, so I get up and dance with him.

We get to the dance floor and I shout, "I don't know how to do this kind of dancing," but he nods confidently.

"I'll teach you," he says, taking one of my hands and putting the other on his shoulder. His other hand comes to my hip, and he starts to move. I try to follow him, but I feel unsure.

"It's okay," he encourages. "Just do what I do." I try to just focus on his face and let my body respond, but I'm not getting clear signals, so I step the wrong way. It's not fun at first, although the music is great and I try to laugh and not take it too seriously. After a while, I get the hang of it. Finally, the song ends and we turn to see that our food is here.

When I get back to the table, a rich rice dish with fresh vegetables in a red sauce is waiting for me, alive with fresh herbs. Starbucks got a beef dish with green olives and red peppers. I should be famished, but somehow, I can't eat. The memory of dancing with Charm at the Beyoncé concert keeps coming back to me.

"You alright? Is your food okay?"

"Everything is wonderful," I say truthfully. "It's just really filling."

He wants to know everything. How do I make decisions? How am I with money? Do I want kids? Do I like to cook? Am I a neat person or a messy person? Do I have plans to go back and get certification so I can be a social worker? Would I ever want to be an entrepreneur?

Whoa. I can appreciate that he's straightforward and wants to get it out on the table, but I feel like I'm being grilled for an executive position. I'm answering in a way that obviously meets his criteria, but what do you do when answering Mr. Right's questions leads you to discover that you're Ms. Wrong for him?

You order ice cream, that's what you do. I'm not even hungry, and Starbucks doesn't have much of a sweet tooth so I take a few bites, and it's doing the trick. He pays the bill, and we take a long walk, talk about our dreams and aspirations. Then we hop back in his car; I notice that he did not tip the valet. As he parks outside my building, he explains he's just getting to a place where he feels like he can seriously date again. The first time we met, he was coming out of a five-year relationship.

I see where he's heading. He's hinting that I'm the woman he is thinking about dating. I'm polite, and frankly, I'm flattered, but I'd be lying if I said I had mutual feelings.

Dreamer, who is the angel at the moment, whispers into my ear, "Poor Starbucks. How do you think he would feel if he knew?"

"Shh," I tell her under my breath.

I thank him for an amazing evening, he walks me to my door, and we kiss. I say good night, feeling nothing at all. Except maybe a little embarrassment that I thought I could so easily slip someone else into Charm's place.

Now I know, that experiment failed. Starbucks is going to make a really wonderful husband to some special lady. But she isn't me. I'd be bored to tears.

My mom once told me I should marry the guy that's crazy about me. "He will spend his whole life trying to make you happy," she said. "If you're crazy about him, you will be the one working to make him happy."

Starbucks is that guy who falls for a woman and thinks she can do no wrong, he scatters rose petals in front of her, and everyone tells her he's "the one." But somehow, all that pandering is a turnoff. It feels lopsided. It's like he has a list, and I check all the boxes on the list, but there's no chemistry.

Seriously, is there something wrong with me, that I can't settle for a "real man" who would go out of his way to make me happy for the rest of my life?

Instead, I'm heartbroken over a guy who can't commit, who has all this other stuff going on, who says he cares but disappears? Yep. Must be something wrong with me.

9:41 P.M.

    Stay Woke: How'd it go?

    Me: It was fun! I'm glad I went.

    Dreamer: Hmph.

    Me: I mean, I don't think I'm ready to seriously date anyone.

Dreamer: Well, I'm glad you know that much.
Stay Woke: You're better than me, I'd have that boy wrapped around my acrylic. But, good for you, you deserve someone to treat you nice for a change.
Me: He did, we had great food, great conversation, he even showed me a few dance moves.
Dreamer: I just hope you don't jump the gun.
Me: No, I learned my lesson. He's a great guy, but we aren't right for each other.

I'm so tired, and of course now I'm craving that Cuban food I didn't eat earlier. Why didn't I get a to-go box?

Before heading to bed, I turn off my phone and charge it in the living room. Otherwise, I will have one ear cocked all night, waiting for Charm to call.

CHAPTER SIX

MONDAY

5:17 A.M.

It's another grey day, with dark clouds gathering in the sky. Why am I outside this early in the morning? I hear a *tick-tick-tick*. I look down, and I am seated in a roller coaster, an old-school wood assembly with painted cars.

I'm the only one on the ride. The coaster is climbing a big hill, the *tick-tick* gets louder. I'm excited! This is going to be fun!

My fists are clenched around the safety bar as the coaster crests the peak — just as it starts to rain.

It's pouring, and I'm dropping, that crazy feeling of gravity misbehaving. I'm soaked to the bone and freezing, and I'm laughing every time the ride goes up, and crying every time it goes down. I want to get off this ride, but I can't.

7:22 A.M.

What a dream! My teeth were actually chattering when I got into the shower. Now I'm crouched over a cup of coffee in front of my laptop as Charlie crunches his food and wags his tail. What is it with me and coffee lately?

Despite my weekend-long social media search, I did not check my email at all, and now, I will pay the price. My inbox is flooded with junk, making this early Monday all that much more Mondayish.

There is a message from an open call I submitted to so long ago, I can't even remember who the publisher was or what I submitted.

Oh please no. Not another rejection, not today. Big sigh. *It's okay, this is what happens if you are a writer. Some of the best writers out there got rejected —*

I stop with the self-talk when I read:

"Congratulations! Your story has been selected to appear in 'Chicken Soup for the Soul: My Amazing Mom.' The book is now on its way to the printer! Thank you for helping us share happiness, inspiration and wellness in this book by allowing us to publish your story. Stay tuned, we'll be sending you more information about the book's release date."

Guess my coaster is climbing another peak!

It was not much of a stretch for me to become a writer — my mom is an English and art teacher. She is going to lose her mind.

Oh. Dear. Lord. Mom.

I panic, scoop up my phone, and tell Siri: "Call Mom, now!" Good thing she is an early bird.

Click, "Hi, Honey!

"Mom, I am so sorry, I said I would call."

"You did, Honey, we talked on Friday. You don't remember?"

"Uh, oh yeah." See what I mean about Friday? It's just gone, blip. "Anyway, you know that story I wrote about you, the Chicken Soup thing?"

"How could I forget? I was the star!" she laughs, as I hear her paintbrush in the background.

I rev up first, "They are going to publish it! Eeeeeeee!"

"Eeeeeeeee!" Gushing ensues.

Let's pause here so I can describe to you my childhood. My mom still lives in my childhood home, but let's go back to 1999: Our house is your classic, single-family home with the shingle siding and a weather vane. In the driveway sits a whale-sized van that regularly carried such a heavy load, its belly practically dragged on the ground. That's where my siblings and I spent countless days cruising to the pool or the library, and of course school. But on the way, inevitably, my mom would spot something on the street and holler, "Wow, look at that, kids, hold tight!" All eight of us, and probably some friends, suddenly piled onto each other while my mom made a U-turn.

If there *were* friends in the car, this is where the real embarrassment began. "What's your mom stopping for?" one of them would ask. We'd look at each other sheepishly. "She saw something she likes," one of us would try to downplay.

Mom would pop the far back and hold up some abandoned piece of, well, garbage as though she just discovered a lost artifact from the pyramids.

"Can you believe this?" she would exclaim.

"Mom, can we just go to the pool?" someone would whine.

Anyway, back to the house. Let's go inside.

The walls are nutty colors in the kitchen and living room, which doubles as her workspace. It wasn't until I was an adult that I realized every night after we went to bed, she would do the dishes then spread out her materials and transform some rickety old stool into a tiny throne. Then she would diligently clean it all up so we had somewhere to eat breakfast the next day.

Why didn't she use the garage, you ask? Well, open the door and you'll find boxes, carts, shelves and drawers filled with art teacher paper, paints, markers, paper mache, you name it. It's fine, the minivan wouldn't fit in here anyway.

I was surrounded by books and filled countless notebooks by the time my first grade teacher taught subjects and nouns. Storytelling was a huge part of my childhood. As you can imagine, that house was loud. There was always someone dancing, or playing freeze tag, or arguing over a toy. So to be in my little corner, in my own imagination? That was the best.

I probably should have chosen communications, or marketing, or English. But I chose social work. I didn't see writing as a real job. In fact, it still seems so far away.

After struggling to stay focused long enough to finish college, I took a year off to "find myself." Three years later, I am still looking. But in the meantime, I made mistakes, shared laughter and "spilled a ton of salt!" I worked on my relationships with my community, and after sharing my experiences with friends and hearing them say, "You should write this down," I finally decided to listen to them (and my mom this whole lifetime) and get it on the page. I started blogging, even calling my blog, "Spill The Salt."

"Candace, this is so exciting, I'm really so proud of you!"

"Thanks, Mom. It was a good story because of you."

"Aw!" I can hear her getting choked up, and I'm choking up too.

After I get off the phone, I spin around the room! They want to publish my story!

My heart floats after days of being a dead weight.

And the first person I want to tell after my Mom is…of course…

The old him, the Charm I Thought I Knew, he who would have been thrilled for me. He read my work at the church and on my blog, and we talked about it. I'd even get his opinion on things when I wanteded a man's perspective.

If he were here right now, he would tell me that this was the first of many acceptances. He would say I should get used to it.

"What are you going to wear when Oprah has you on?" I would laugh and give him a playful shove. "Seriously. You're on your way." I feel another moment of sadness.

No, uh-uh. I'm not going to let this ruin my victory. I know one story in one book is just a step, but it feels huge. It feels like a sign.

7:54 A.M.

> Dreamer: WHAAAAA?! Girl, I am SO PROUD OF YOU!!
> (Insert all kinds of emojis)
> Stay Woke: Candace, that is amazing!! You are going to be in print, Lady! Your dream is coming true!

And then it starts up again.

> Dreamer: Oh now you HAVE to call Charm and tell him. Come on, he is your biggest supporter! Why wouldn't you call him? I know he'd be proud of you. And so happy to hear from you. You know it doesn't hurt to reach out first, Candace. It doesn't make you look weak. The one to reach out first is actually the most courageous.
> Stay Woke: Uh-uh. This is your win... you owe him NOTHING! He can find out about the book with the rest of the general population. I wouldn't even sign a copy for his mama! Nope. Don't call, Girl, stay strong. And when you blow up, don't look back!

Now I'm even more torn. And they have reversed roles again: Stay Woke is playing the angel, and Dreamer is playing the devil. Their advice makes a lot of sense (most of the time!), but I still can't help but feel like this win would be so much sweeter if he knew.

Maybe I should call …

> Stay Woke: Candace, I can hear those gears grinding, Girl, DO NOT CALL.

Dang, she is good, right?

> Dreamer: This could be the thing that brings you back together!

Oh Dreamer, always the idealist.

> Stay Woke: She does not need that bagabond. Watch, in a year, she will be dating Michael B. Jordan.
>
> Dreamer: LOL
>
> Me: LOL

8:56 A.M.

I arrive at work full of fire. Shelley sees me blow in from across the room, and she can tell by the look on my face that something is up.

"What's up?" she zooms in.

I tell her the good news and immediately there is a small swarm of co-workers around me exclaiming, "Good for you!" and "When can we read it?" and "Wait, you're a writer?" I try to be gracious about the praise, but honestly, the sudden attention feels awkward.

Nonetheless, I'm glowing when I sit down and settle in, and then I boot up my computer and my heart sinks. I never wanted to write so badly in my life than at this moment. I should be writing books!

I don't want to do this job anymore. Don't get me wrong, I like it here. It's a decent job with great people, it's work I can feel good about (helping people with their money), but it's not my life's work, it's just a job.

Here I am, 29, a useless degree in social work because you have to do a billion hours of interning before you can actually certify as a social worker. I'm a bank clerk, single, and I want to be a writer? For a living?

Every time I sit down at my desk now and open up a spreadsheet, I think about all I could be accomplishing with my writing — working on my blog, or even creative ideas that help the church. It's an itch deep inside of me, and no matter how hard I concentrate, there is always a part of my soul that feels like I should be writing.

This requires deep breaths. Reset my thinking. There is still a long road ahead.

4:19 P.M.
The girls have been blowing up my phone all day. They are so sweet, aren't they? I've been hiding the phone under my desk and texting back when I can. They want to take me to dinner tomorrow. Well, ok! A celebratory dinner with my girls, that sounds perfect.

But every time I look down at the phone, one name doesn't appear. It lights me up, frankly, this big fat news, this validation that all the writing I've been doing has finally paid off.

7:27 P.M.
Back at home, I'm practicing my acceptance speech at the Ebony Awards for the Best 20-Something Romantic Comedy Memoir category. A girl can dream can't she? I'm also going through my closet tossing old shoes, dresses and blouses I haven't worn in ages. I will not be needing these ratty old off-brand suits anymore. Hmm I wonder, what does one wear to one's first book signing?

After some quick social media stalking (for once Charm's feed is silent, which in and of itself is strange), I get back to my blog and do a little victory lap about the "Chicken Soup for the Soul" acceptance letter. I realize I don't actually know much about how this works. Will I get paid? Will I get a copy? I start digging to figure out how this whole publishing process goes.

Oh. I do get paid. This is awesome. All this feels like going down a rabbit hole — there is so much I don't know! I make myself a list of things I need to research and promise myself that this is part of my professional life now, and I need to do my homework.

10:18 P.M.
Still no word from him. I think about posting something on Facebook, then decide against it. I'd just agonize if he saw it and chose not to say anything, or didn't see it, or saw it and used it as an excuse to call...

I should just call him and tell him. What is the big deal? I'm making a mountain out of an anthill. Time for an episode of *"Sex in the City."* Then my phone goes off. I dash over to it. It's the girls again.

> Stay Woke: I saw you were on Facebook, but you didn't post anything about the book?
> Dreamer: I was surprised by that too! Not like you not to brag a little. ;)
> Me: Oh, it just felt like I'd be signaling to Charm, and then I thought what if he ignores it, and then I thought I should just call him.
> Dreamer: Yes! Sing it from the mountaintops, Candace! You should tell him about your success!
> Stay Woke: HEEEEELLLL NO. Don't call. But do post it! Don't let him ruin this! It's your thing...

I tune out. This whole breaking up thing is exhausting. All this processing. Suddenly, my bed swallows me whole.

CHAPTER SEVEN

TUESDAY

7:12 A.M.
No crazy dreams. Slept right through. I'm going to make it. I'm an author, dang it, I've got bigger fish to fry than to worry about that dude. I get up, eat a bowl of cereal and blog for 20 minutes. It's better than nothing.

This small-minded track is not working. Time to think big. Determination, that's what I need!

I add to my mental list of things I need to look into: finding a writer's workshop nearby, maybe taking an online creative writing class, searching through my Word drafts to figure out what I need to work on next. Yes, this is good, putting energy someplace where it will pay off.

8:46 A.M
And they pick right back up where they left off last night:

> Stay Woke: What are you doing? You went ghost last night. You better not be thinking about calling that little

boy. Dreamer and I made reservations, let's go out and celebrate, Miss Bestselling Author! I'm ready to paint the city red and I don't care that it's a Tuesday! Be ready at 7.
Me: Well, if you insist!
Dreamer: We do!

I have had some casual contact with Starbucks, nothing worth mentioning. I've gone from feeling hopeful to just plain feeling sorry for the guy. I hesitate to tell him about the acceptance because I know it would be a pretext for us going out again. I can't help but listen to Dreamer's words that it's self-serving to go out with him when it's going nowhere. Finally, I just send him a message saying just that: I'm not ready, and he needs someone who is just as excited about falling in love as he is. He was surprisingly understanding, I guess that's what a divorce will do for you. We said we'd stay in touch, and he wished me the best of luck.

Stay Woke insists she pick me up because she knows if she doesn't, I probably won't go, and then, I'll get into more shopping trouble. As much as I enjoy shopping for shoes, my credit card can't take another mall run or online jag.

Who am I kidding, what else would I be doing? Out with the girls it is. We always have such a good time. I know they're really happy for me. It's difficult to find one friend who sincerely wants you to do well. I'm lucky enough to have found two. Dreamer encouraged me to start my blog. She swears that I'm the funniest person she knows (even though I don't agree) and that she should not be the only person entertained by my stories. After years of convincing, I stepped up and gave it a shot. Now, writing is like breathing — it comes so naturally. That day, she became my brand consultant. She designs every flier, she listens to every idea and she keeps me focused when I get off track.

Stay Woke has been there since day 1. The first time she heard me complain about the initial startup cost to launch the website, she stood there with her checkbook in hand.

"How much do you need?"

"No," I waved her away, "it's really sweet of you…"

Stay Woke was already on a call to Dreamer. I tried to object, but she held up a finger.

"How much does that stubborn heifer need?" Those were her exact words. I fell out laughing. Dreamer told me later that she gave Stay Woke the exact dollar amount for the website, and then Stay Woke doubled it! My own personal dream team. Thank God for friends.

6:28 P.M.

There was no way Stay Woke was going to arrive at the time she promised. She would be early, and I would not be ready, and she would sit on the bed and watch me explore my outfit options.

"Yeeeessssss," I tell her. She's wearing this vivid green turtleneck that sets off her big brown eyes.

"Why thank you," she replies. "Now, does the word reservation mean anything to you? This is Townhouse woman. If we're late, they'll give our table away. I had to pay my sitter double just to make this night happen."

I pay her no mind. I've heard this speech several times before, and I know her well enough that if she says our reservation is at 7:00 it's really at 8:00. And I want to look really nice. I pull out a blue dress. It's cute, but feels a little businessy. I find another one, a hip hugging floral number.

"Yes!" she points. I try it on with peek toe Marilyn Monroe-style heels.

"You look really nice," she says, like she's reading my mind. "Now, let's GO."

7:00 P.M.

You could describe the style of Townhouse in Detroit as "classy heavy industry." It has a glass ceiling, brick walls and those dangling bare bulbs that make the room look warm. Dreamer is already here. Her navy pencil skirt and flowy peach shirt complement her skin and figure perfectly. It's obvious she left her blazer in the car because she dresses like the CEO of a Fortune 500 company daily. At least Stay Woke also got the memo, in her figure-hugging turtleneck dress. Her jewelry sparkles like the restaurant lights, and her heels are nearly as high as mine.

Here is where my girls are in lock step: They both think if you are on time, you are actually late. I personally believe in flex time, I need a range! My time management drives my girls crazy.

Dreamer has her phone in one hand and a pen writing in a notepad in the other. When she sees us approach she quickly stashes them, "It's about time you two made it. I started to order without you," she jokes as she jumped up for hugs. We create a little huddle and cheer together, our high heels the only thing preventing us from actually jumping up and down. They gush over me again, and it feels so good, my heart melts.

Dreamer usually wouldn't order anything but water until we arrived. She's a firm believer in "etiquette," and starting a celebration without the guest of honor is a big "no-no." However, her timing is perfect, because as soon as we sit down, the appetizers appear like magic.

I am determined to savor this meal, and it's about time because my relationship with food had suffered. Immediately, we all have a mouthful of calamari. "Um more of this, yes please." My eye drifts over the menu to see if anything compares to the rice dish I had at Vicente's.

Oh, these rosemary garlic lamb chops sounds delish. I look up at my two pretty lady friends who are perusing their own menus and discussing. I tell them about waking up from the roller coaster dream, how I was feeling so low and then I got the email from "Chicken Soup."

"The Lord works in mysterious ways," Dreamer says.

"Yes indeed," Stay Woke agrees, and she lifts her glass and says, "To Candace."

Dreamer echoes, "To Candace." I'm blushing when I raise my ice tea to toast. I'm so glad I came out — I'm bursting. The laughs alone make it worth it.

"So how is it going with that guy you're seeing?" Dreamer asks Stay Woke.

"Oh," she rolls her eyes. "Kicked to the curb because he had 'momma's boy issues.' " She takes a sip of her wine and continues. "He had to cancel our last date because his mom needed a ride to church." Dreamer and I exchange a look that goes something like, "Why does that make him a momma's boy? That's a good man, right?"

Stay Woke sees us looking and finishes the bite in her mouth before she jumps in with, "It was the fourth time he did this!" She launches into an impression of him talking in a nerdy voice. " 'Uh, Stay Woke, yeah sorry, I have to cancel our date again. Yes, Mother needs a ride to church. No, I guess she just wants me to stay there and wait for her. Sorry bout that. Can we reschedule?' " The tension breaks up with laughter at the idea that this grown man doesn't know how to plan his dates around his mom's church schedule. We all know that either he's a momma's boy, or he's using his momma as an excuse, and neither is an acceptable quality in a man.

Two handsome waiters arrive with steaming, piping hot plates of food. We ooh and aah and take up our forks. I can honestly say that the company, the food and the room were simply divine.

Now it's Dreamer's turn. It's the usual: Her man is busy, she is busy, between work, the house and the family, when do they ever have time for each other? She's raising her stepson as if he's her own, but she really wants a birth child too. Mr. Dreamer is now notorious for finding ways of avoiding the topic of baby number two.

"At least he's paying the bills and raising a good son," I point out. Her boy is so smart, his private school education is paying off.

"Amen to that," Dreamer lifts her glass. "But my maternal clock is ticking, and he's constantly walking around going, 'I don't hear anything, do you?' "

Stay Woke hits the nail on the head. "He's spoiled and doesn't want to have to share Dreamer with a child." Dreamer is a natural mother, and I get it that she wants to experience birth and all that. Me, I'm so far away from it, I can't even think about kids yet.

Look at us, I think to myself. *We are all intelligent, educated, hardworking, loving women. Why is it so hard for us to get what we need from men? Are we expecting too much? Or is it that men simply don't have it in them?* Of course my mind wanders back to Charm, and I absently check my phone until Stay Woke notices me, interrupting Dreamer in mid-sentence, "CANDACE, LET IT GO!"

"Uh, I was just —" Now it's Stay Woke and Dreamer's turn to exchange looks.

"Girl, I love you and someone has to say it," Stay Woke starts. "You need to let it go. He has. I know you're not sleeping, and you're a wreck waiting for him to circle back." I can't exactly argue. "You are looking at this all wrong: He did you a favor! Did you forget you wanted to break up with him?"

"I can't lie, you did say that," Dreamer admits reluctantly.

"You were tired of his crap. It's just your ego that's smarting right now because he dumped you and not the other way around. It wasn't working for you, and he was hiding something, I just know it."

Dreamer is suddenly very interested at something across the room as she takes a sip of her drink. I narrow my eyes and wait for her to look back in my direction. *Who's wearing the wings, and who's carrying the pitchfork tonight, Ladies?* I'm wondering.

Finally, Dreamer looks back in my direction and says, "Okay. Yes, I advocated for him. It was just because when you were good, you were really, really good together." She leans in, like she's closing the deal. "He was doing all that work at the church, he was supporting your writing, you made a good team." At this point, Stay Woke shrugs like, yeah, so what.

"However, sis is right," Dreamer nods toward Stay Woke. This is a crazy moment because for once my girls aren't opposing planets orbiting around me. For once, they are unified. "Now that I think about it, he did all that good stuff when you were friends, and he started to fall off when y'all started dating." A ton a bricks like only your two best friends can drop together.

"It's been a week," Stay Woke says, trying to pull the plane up, "and look how much you've accomplished, even in the middle of nursing a broken heart! You are still young, Candace, at the beginning of your adult life, and you are going to meet a lot of people through your new career. Your REAL career as a writer!"

Now this was not the first or even the fourth thought that passed through my mind when I got that acceptance letter. But Stay Woke is again right. I need to seize this opportunity, connect to other writers, start going to events, stuff that writers do. Also, the actual writing part. On top of everything else, the muse seems to have flown the coop.

We all look down at our plates, and we might as well have licked them clean. Dreamer bats her eyes at our waiter who kindly takes our plates and offers us desert menus. Over a flourless chocolate skillet brownie, we remind each other that we are all on a journey, and we are lucky we have each other.

11:25 P.M.
I'm at home, in my comfy clothes, my face washed, my Charlie in my lap. I look out at the city lights and think about what Dreamer and Stay Woke said.

I need to let go. I was genuinely in love with Charm, and for whatever reason, reasons I know, or reasons that haven't even occurred to me, he doesn't return that love, even if that love is just friendship. So I need to let go twice: once for the romance, and again for the friendship.

My girls, on the other hand, love me, and everything they do and say is all out of love. I'm reliving the flavors and laughter, and thanking God for these truly blessed moments.

Without warning, I'm consumed with the need to write something down. Move, Charlie, where's my pen. Ah.

What will I write next, in this new, electric chapter of my life?

CHAPTER EIGHT

WEDNESDAY

10:15 A.M.
Yes, here I am at work again. Butt in the chair. Big dreams. I contemplate quitting as Jean and Shelley stand in front of my desk and chat my ear off about the difference in prices at Wal-Mart versus Home Depot. Okay, that's a bit of an exaggeration. But today is as stiff as an old wig. Wednesdays are bad enough, but now it has been exactly a week since you-know-who did you-know-what. My normal routine is a reminder that my normal routine has a big hole in it. Also, Bible Study. I can't even right now.

And then, it happens.

"Candace, are you going to bring Charm to the office get-together?" Jean peers at me with a look so focused, I can feel the little red bead of her laser sight on my forehead. Too late to lie.

"We aren't dating anymore." At once, Jean and Shelley are at my side consoling me, asking all kinds of questions and saying uncomfortable stuff like, "Oh you poor thing!"

It's like when you bang your head, and it doesn't hurt at first, but someone saw it and the look on their face is so severe that all the sudden, your head hurts.

Jean and Shelley won't stop talking. They even rope in another employee I don't know. My head hurts. I stayed out a little too late with the girls last night, and I could practically fall asleep on my feet.

"I'm fine, no really, I'm fine," I say with enough force that Jean, Shelley and the other woman scatter like pigeons.

I say a prayer of thanks that I do not drink and that being hungover is not one of my problems. It's okay, I tell myself, at least there is a three-day weekend coming up. This would usually be an opportunity to do something fun with Charm. But that's okay.

I'm going to write, I'm going to exercise, I'm going to shop for groceries and cook food for a change. And I'm going to write. No really. I am.

It's been a week. The resolve I felt last night after hearing from Dreamer and Stay Woke is starting to slip. My mind is still trying to work around the problem like a politician looking for a loophole.

Should I call him to let him know we are officially done?
I need closure.
Should I brag about Chicken Soup publishing my work?
How much longer will I have to live like this? I'm miserable.
I should just go ahead and call.
It's just a conversation.
I miss the friendship!
I mean, I'm not perfect either.
Leverage. By calling, I'm the bigger person, right?

11:31 A.M.

"So in short, I want to close that account and open another account, move the money from the first account, that you are going to close, to the one that you are going to open, and then also set up a savings account that will automatically deduct my taxes from my paycheck and deposit them into the savings. Did you get all that?"

A crabby old man is seated at my desk making absolutely no sense. The only upside is, he might make a good character in a story someday.

As I patiently explain to this customer why what he wants to do doesn't make sense, my mind wanders again. This time, I'm picturing Charm lounging on his couch with yet another version of Ms. Look-at-Me. They are watching TV, all cuddled up, laughing at the jokes. She is wearing 6-inch, clear heels, if that tells you anything. In my imagination, his phone buzzes and he looks down at the screen and sees my number.

"Who's that?" Ms. Look-at-Me asks.

"That's nobody, Baby," he deletes my number with a smile and proceeds to make out with Ms. Look-at-Me, who takes a selfie for good measure.

5:16 P.M.

An accident on my way home makes my drive extremely long. The echo of my R&B music bounces off my windows, noise I need to drown my thoughts. It's raining, and an oldie-but-goodie comes on the radio.

"My love must be a kind of blind love," I sing along. The commuters in the other cars join in: "shoo-bop-shoo-bop." The water droplets on the window shield remind me of a slowly turning disco ball, throwing light.

I chuckle when the semi-truck driver starts swaying behind his steering wheel. The piano chords beat in time to the raindrops. "I can't see anyone but you."

"Shoo-bop-shoo-bop."

The cars creep forward almost in a dance.

"I only have eyes, for yooooouuuu…"

The windshield wipers mimic the sound of the brushes on the drums. I remember the first time he told me he loved me. It was days after that conversation in his truck after the movie. He asked me to look at something for one of his classes, so I came over that night. I was sitting at his desk, looking at the paper he was writing on the screen, fixing his grammar, making some little changes, when he came up behind me and wrapped his arms around me.

"I love you," he whispered in my ear. Probably not an accident I ended up completely rewriting that paper for him. And he got an A.

"All the stars," croons the radio, "are out tonight, but I can't tell if it's cloudy or bright."

Did he mean it? Was there ever actually love in his heart for me, or was I just a sucker he could use for his own gain?

I glance at my phone. I've got to stop believing this guy is the only guy in the world.

6:12 P.M.

Thank God, home to an anxious dog, but no poop. He's pleased with himself, I can tell. We go for a quick turn around the block and come home.

I get into my comfy clothes and open the fridge. Nothing but some condiments, a bubbly water and some celery that is so old and yellow, it could pass for bamboo.

Tomorrow after work, I am determined to go to a grocery store, take food off the shelves, pay for it, and bring it home and eat it. *This is nuts*, I think as I open my cabinets and find more nothing. I used to make that jerk a home-cooked meal almost every day. There were times when he was so broke, I was his meal ticket. But somehow, I'm the one who's spoiled?

It's been a week since I made a meal. I can't believe this. Chinese takeout it is. Again.

I make the call, throw on a sweatshirt, and why not, come on, Charlie. He can't believe it, another walk! He's the luckiest little dog in the whole world!

I'm getting used to this, I realize once the fresh air hits me.

Day ten has got to be better than this. Only three more days. By day ten, I'll be completely over him. This is all just part of the breaking up process. I will totally move on in another couple days. I think. I hope.

After some veggie chow mein and reading, I head to the bedroom to change my sheets. I'm sitting on the edge of my bed, admiring my fresh linen, when my phone bleeps. Four missed calls. I must have forgotten to turn my ringer back on.

My stomach binds into knots instantly when I see "CHARM" appear on the screen. He tried to call twice. I drop the phone on the bed and walk around the room, talking to myself. "What do I do? I've been waiting for this call for five days and now, NOW, that I've really come to grips with the idea we're done, he calls?"

Wait, I think to myself as I do laps around my apartment. There could be all kinds of reasons he's calling me.

SCENARIO 1:
CHARM
Wearing a Hugo Boss suit with Mrs. Look-at-Me in the background admiring a huge rock on her finger.
Hey Candace, I just wanted to be the one to tell you, I'm engaged! I hope you'll come to the wedding?

SCENARIO 2:

CHARM

Wearing a white robe with a medallion around his neck and massage music in the background.

Candace, I've been so wrong, I'm seeing a counselor, started medicating, and I wanted to say thank you. I'm on my way to an ashram in India to be closer to God. I couldn't have seen the Light without you.

SCENARIO 3:

CHARM

Dressed normally in his apartment.

Oh sorry, my bad. That was a butt dial. Both times.

7:28 P.M.

Ugh.

I'm still staring at the screen as if I can decode the intent behind his calls. I want to answer. But I shouldn't.

How entitled! To dump me in a text and wait a week. What does he think, I've just been waiting around for this call?

Don't say it, Reader.

I'm chewing my nails. I could actually bite my hand off. What do I do? I'm afraid to reach out to my girls after all the effort they've put in. I know what they would say, and I'm not even going to ask.

So I pray. *God, what is this about? What am I supposed to be learning here? Should I give him an audience?* At that moment, a flood of memories pours into my mind: his smell, his secrets, all the fun we had.

Am I being too hard on him?

Gulping some water. I think of that Erykah Badu song, *"tried to turn the sauna up to hotter, drank whole jar of holy water, but it won't let go…"*

I try writing down my feelings, but they come out all jumbled, like the dog hair that builds up under the furniture. Maybe I will just wait and return his call tomorrow? Or send him a text, something casual, like I'm not that bothered. Yeah. That's a good plan.

9:14 P.M.
Then the phone rings again. Caller ID tells me it's him. That's three calls in one night.

I feel like a little girl sitting at a table full of sweets, and all the grownups are telling me, "Candace, now don't you touch those cookies, you have to wait."

Ooh, I pin my hands under my legs, but that cookie, it looks so freakin' good. I try but my hand just goes out, and I'm watching myself reach for it, like no, don't do it —

"Hello?"

"Hey, Beautiful."

Uh. I flop on my bed. There he is. Totally unaware of all I've been through this last week. Silence fills in the space between us.

"So how have you been?" he asks. So casual.

"Good." Total lie, but there is no way I'm telling the truth. Another silence.

"Well, that's good," he tries. "I've been thinking about you, just, I don't know, seemed like we needed some space." I say nothing. It's like we are playing phone chicken. Who's going to talk first?

"Hello?" he asks after the line is dead quiet for minutes.

"Yeah, I'm here."

He tells me: "It feels strange, not hearing your voice every day."

"But that was your idea. That's how you wanted it." I'm incapable of taking the edge out of my voice.

"No. I never wanted that. I really love having you in my life, Candace."

My heart is swimming in lava while the hard, cold shell of me melts. He keeps talking, just filling the space. "I went to Aaron's game last Friday. He won, I was so proud." He was such a good uncle to that little kid, always practicing with him and encouraging him. "First person I wanted to tell was you."

Still, I say nothing. His words are a seductive melody.

A funny image pops into my head, of Charm wearing a turban, playing the flute so sweetly. And I'm the cobra, in attack pose, ready to strike, but then I start swaying to the warm, sad tones of his flute…

"I had a flat tire last week, had to replace them all. Oh and…" He pauses like he wants to build the drama, "I didn't get that promotion."

"What?" This takes me by complete surprise. He had put in some serious hours trying to impress management at his office. I even proofed some of his work to make sure it was flawless. Hard to believe they gave it to someone else.

"Yeah," he says.

"I'm sorry," I say truthfully. "I know how much you wanted that."

And then, something inside me snaps and I blurt it out: "I got an acceptance letter from the 'Chicken Soup for the Soul' publishers. They want my story."

Now why did I just do that? It's his turn to be silent. Then he laughs, "Candace, why didn't you tell me that first?"

Hello…were you not present the last time we talked? Don't you remember dumping me? How could I? And besides, was your phone broken? You should've been the one to call me!

He's still going. "This is a HUGE deal!"

"Yeah, feels really good," I admit. Dang, what am I, an open book now?

"Please let me celebrate with you. It would mean so much to me. You've worked so hard, we gotta celebrate."

"I don't know. I'm really confused." Yep, my book is wide open.

"I am too," he says, like he's trying to comfort me, which is just weird. "I wanted to reach out, but I didn't because I thought you were upset. I just…sometimes I feel like I can't give you everything you need," I feel myself convulse and he probably senses it because he hurries up with, "everything you *deserve.*"

"None of this was my idea!" I sputter, unable to hold it in, "we were friends! It was good! And you, you —"

"Can't we still be friends?" he says, cutting me off. "That's what you said in our last conversation, right?"

He has me there. I did say that. "Yes," I say primly.

"So then why wouldn't you call me?"

Wow, did you see what he just did just now, how he flipped the script? Charm knows me better than anyone. He had to know that I could not push a button and revert back to being his friend. I'm not a robot. And I have my pride.

"Candace," he slips around to another angle, playing that music again. "I don't want to lose you. You're *in my life.* Please don't be mad at me. Let me celebrate this achievement with you."

My bed feels like a boat and I'm a shipwreck survivor, floating out at sea. How could he even ask me? I'm not ready. What does he expect? For us to pick up where we left off? He's the one who allowed seconds to turn to minutes and minutes to turn to hours and hours into days. And now it's been eight to be exact. No, I can't just pick up where we left off. No, I'm not ready.

"I'm not asking you to be back together, all I'm saying is for us to celebrate."

"I know that's what you're asking. I just don't think I can go back to the way things were."

"I'm not asking for that either. I know we need some time to readjust. Think about it, you don't have to decide right now."

"I'll sleep on it and then I'll let you know."

"Can we talk a little longer?"

Could this be my life again? Like I'm just not getting my first choice, so now I'm sour grapes and I'm going to ruin our beautiful friendship? Dreamer says when we are hurt, we don't consider that the other person is hurting too. We just get wrapped up in our own pain. At this moment, does it matter that he was the one who ended things? A breakup is a breakup, and I actually believe him, that what he is able to give and what I need are two different things.

The Dreamer in me wants to show him compassion. But the Stay Woke in me realizes this could all be part of the game to get back into my head, and play me that sweet tune.

11:37 P.M.

My thoughts are all over the place. I'm really confused. Why am I still here, listening to him talk like he didn't ditch me in a text and now he's acting as if nothing happened? He's telling me a story. I'm not even paying attention, because I don't even know what I want anymore. I want him, I know that, but with him comes more secrets, more inconsistency, more lashing out and more apologies. This cycle of disappointment and confrontation and temporary fixes.

He must sense that my mind is elsewhere. "Look, I've made some mistakes," he admits. "I don't always know how to handle these types of things. You know that about me. But I care about you. And I know how much this means to you, and I'm proud of you."

He's still trying to get me to let him back in, and I'm frozen. That little girl part of me is screaming, yes, yes, YES give me the cookie! But my Pride butts in like, oh no, it can't be that easy! I'm not buying it. So now there is a full-blown argument in my head. I'm pretty sure there is a cat lady in there somewhere sitting in her rocker saying, *I just miss my best friend.*

He was my champion, there for every celebration since we became friends. He was always the first to get up and do a victory dance when monumental events happened in my life. And so, of course, it brought me immense joy to participate in his life. We showed up for each other.

"Candace?"

I got this. I can pivot. I rationalize like mad: How do I know if this will do more damage than good unless I see him again? This is all I've been wanting, and now it's here. I've been a wreck, I'll admit it. It's been tough. But what doesn't kill you makes you stronger, right? I'm tough. I'm stronger.

"Alright," I hear myself say, but my voice sounds far away.

"Alright!" he says with that same enthusiasm that made me fall for him in the first place.

CHAPTER NINE

THURSDAY

1:04 A.M.

I tried to get off the phone earlier, really, I did. By the time I accomplished what should've been a simple task, the start of a new day approached.

As usual, our conversations just flowed, like being in a warm bath. Even though I said I wanted to get off the phone, deep down I didn't. And he knew it. And so, he didn't let me. We talked, laughed, I fought back tears at a few points and he remained "cool."

But saying yes to him felt uncomfortable too. I said I wouldn't go back. That I would move on. That I would let go. I made a pact with myself and my friends not to get back on the ride. Now I'm a little embarrassed.

He apologizes for being too stubborn to call and for allowing the disappointment of not getting the promotion to keep him distant.

He sounds so sincere. It could happen? Our love is strong enough, right? We had been through so much together. Why would I just throw the towel in? Now he's vowing to change and commit.

"Wait, what do you mean, 'commit?' "

He backpedals, "To our friendship, I mean I'm committed to staying friends."

I'm quiet and then I say doubtfully, "okay."

He sees he has an opportunity to end the conversation on a high note. "I should let you get some sleep."

Sleep? How does one accomplish that? "Yeah, I should go."

"I'll text you tomorrow. Sweet Dreams, Love." And then he hangs up. No he didn't.

I burst into a full cry before I finally fall asleep exhausted.

5:10 A.M.

I'm up to watch the sunrise. Guess I'll sleep when I'm dead. My mind has been flipping like Simone Biles all night. Inventing new moves.

My phone chimes. It's him, of course. Guess he didn't sleep much either. Why do I feel so uncomfortable when I look at the screen and read:

> Charm: I'm glad we talked! I know I was wrong and I know you're scared but give me the opportunity to make it up to you. How about Maggiano's at 8 tonight?

I get up, look at my reflection. It bends and stretches like a fun house mirror. It's day 8. Or did I just reset and go back to zero when I picked up the phone last night? I'm baffled. All my resolve seems to have poured out of me again. I just spent seven hard days trying to come to grips with the fact that my first love wasn't real. Now he's telling me, no, *it is real.*

The feeling of his voice passes through me. Of hearing him say the words: "I'm sorry," and "I care about you." I'm wondering for the millionth time, did I misjudge him?

5:50 A.M.

>Me: Okay.
>
>Charm: Sweet, I'll pick you up, 7:30?
>
>Me: No, I'll meet you there. See you at 8.
>
>Charm: Ok, you sure? I don't mind.
>
>Me: No, it's alright, I'll meet you there.
>
>Charm: Alright. See you then.

3:38 P.M.

I left my phone off all day. I cannot tell the Ladies. Dreamer will cloud my judgment, and Stay Woke will just judge me. And him, but mostly me. God bless them both, but this is between me and myself today.

I check it once. Charm asks again if he can pick me up. I respond, "No, I'll meet you there." I want neutral territory. And I want him to have the long view.

All day, I'm stuck in mental third gear. I actually made some clerical mistakes, which is unlike me. I must be running off of pure adrenaline given that I have had less than four hours of sleep. I could either run a marathon or hibernate. I cut out of work just a speck early so I can get some exercise in before I meet Charm. Maybe I can run some of this energy off.

5:03 A.M.

At the gym, I puff away on the elliptical. I'm remembering why I do not like the gym. It smells like sweat and too much perfume, and it's a regular meat market in here. When women walk by, you can practically see the men making mental notes about which cut of meat they'd like.

I get a good sweat going, and then I settle into the sauna for a minute. Maybe I can detox some of this feeling.

6:42 P.M.

I'm home, showered, in my robe. Charlie is looking at me with that complicated expression, but I'm too busy searching through the closet to find something to wear. Then I pull it out — it's that burgundy silky dress that looks so cute with my strappy gold heels. Oh yes. I pull out the lingerie I just purchased, that lingerie that was supposedly "just for me."

I do my hair and makeup. The dress, I'm sorry, it's bangin.'

"Wish me luck!" I say to Charlie, with no conviction in my voice whatsoever.

He just ducks his head and slinks away.

8:04 P.M.

I forgot that this dress and the Jeep do not get along. After a few tries, I managed to hike up the skirt enough to climb up.

In the parking lot of the restaurant, I give myself a pep talk as I check my face in the rear view. "You can do this," I assure myself. "It's just dinner, between friends."

"Yeah sure," my expression says back to me. "You keep telling yourself that."

I climb out of the Jeep — getting out is much easier — and clop through the parking lot. I know he's already there because I hear my phone beep in my purse. I take deep breaths and spot him in the waiting area. He doesn't see me for a moment, he's looking at his phone, and it gives me a second to look at him. He's wearing a dark brown sweater under a suede jacket that fits him so well. My heart jerks like it's attached to my throat. I open the door, and he looks up.

He stands as I make my way toward him, weaving between the other diners, until I'm standing in front of him. I look up, and our eyes meet. The smile that appears on my face is involuntary.

"You look amazing," the appreciation in his voice is obvious. I try to stay cool, but I'm pretty sure it doesn't work. He opens his arms and I fall into them. Charm. So warm. The sun of his attention just shines down on me.

"It's so good to see you," he whispers in my ear. I shiver as he pulls back.

"Really," he repeats, "you look so great. That color suits you." I smile. We look amazing together.

"Why thank you." The hostess is a pretty young thing who comes over and tells us our table is ready. As she guides us into the restaurant, she asks if we are celebrating anything.

"Yes," Charm doesn't hesitate. "She is a published author."

"Wow!" the hostess is immediately on board. You can tell she is "in love with love." We sit and I see the hostess tell the waitress who comes over and also makes a big deal about my news. Boy, this is really getting around. If this doesn't work out, maybe I should hire Charm to be my publicist.

"I'm ravenous," I say as soon as we are seated. And I am. It's like eight days worth of hunger just showed up at the dinner table, butting in, "mind if we join you?" I picture seven versions of myself at the table with us, sucking down breadsticks and lasagna in an unladylike fashion.

The waitress comes over and asks about drinks. I get my usual, ice tea, and I'm watching Charm closely. He's about to order a Hennessy, I just know it, but he catches me looking and changes his mind.

"You know what, I'm good with water for now." This is unexpected, but I don't reveal that to him.

For some reason, I thought we were going to keep the conversation light, like trying to go back to the friend zone. But that is not Charm's idea. He jumps right into the deep end of the pool.

"I've been thinking a lot. About us. I still feel really bad about what happened." I take up my drink and take a loud sip through the straw. My silence means he has to keep talking.

"I realize I have this habit of folding at the first sign of trouble. Breaking up should never be the solution."

I give him the eyebrow — an expression invented and perfected by black women. It's a cross of "You don't say?" and "I've heard it all before," mixed with a dash of, "I wish I believed you."

"Your opinion matters and I'm going to change."

I look past him at the waitress and gesture to the empty breadbasket on the table.

"Boy, am I hungry!" I exclaim with too much enthusiasm as the second basket of bread arrives.

Reader, meet me over here: I'm skeptical. You tell me: Is he finally hearing me when I tell him he didn't have to disappear for days to get his point across? Or that talking about our issues wasn't the same as arguing? And that just because I voice my needs, it does not mean I'm saying he never does anything right? Why couldn't he have said all this eight days ago? Where were these words when I needed them?

Is this his moment of clarity? He's making some big proclamations. This time was going to be different. I just knew it would be. It had to be. Why would he go through all this trouble to convince me if he didn't really want this too?

Watching him explain, and gesture and convince, it's like the void of the last week just evaporated. Everything I tried so hard not to feel comes rushing back. Can I let go of the boyfriend part and still manage to keep my friend?

We've done it before, haven't we? If it weren't for the friendship we wouldn't even be here. But what about all the intimate love that came out of it. Do we just put that back in the box? Toss it to the side? Act like it didn't exist?

He sees all this on my face and he stops talking. We just look at each other. Time seems to stop.

I thought this was special. This bond between us. Unique. It got us through the toughest of times. I learned so much just through loving him.

"I don't know what you want," I finally say.

"I don't want to lose you," he says again. "I love you, Candace."

Love has taught me a lot the last week. I don't know what I'm doing, but I recognize this feeling. The feeling of being at the center of his universe.

I've watched all my friends find love, get married, embark on adventures together like travel, family, true partnerships that can face adversity. I want my own.

The waitress comes back, and I haven't even looked at the menu. Charm offers to order for us, and I'm grateful because I'm still stuck on this "love of my life" or "hit the road, Jack," decision.

"Tell me more about the book," he says. And I'm relieved for the time being that we can talk about something else. It's this man, who is such a good listener, who is so supportive and positive, who knows all the little details of my life, that I want.

Once upon a time, I thought he was it. Look at him, sitting there across the table from me, his chocolate and tan setting off his skin. He's facing me, leaning in. Like I'm the most important thing in this world. We've been on countless dates. But nothing like this. He's even more open, more confident, and he's never looked better. Is this the same guy who told me in so many words to mind my own damn business?

9:51 P.M.

Was he always this funny? When did he become so funny? I thought the restaurant was going to kick us out for laughing so loud and hard. If it did, I didn't care.

We have already racked up quite the bill, and neither of us are ready to leave. We keep thinking of stuff to order and new topics to discuss. Even when our waitress gives us the "you don't have to leave but my shift is over" line, we remain sitting, making excuses to touch hands and flirt. He cashes out and we keep talking. When the lights brighten and the music stops we decide maybe it is best to not get locked in the place.

He walks me to my car, and we stand outside. The cold Michigan air is still brisk in the spring. My outfit was too cute to wear anything but a little jacket. Charm sees that I'm shivering.

All at once, he envelops me. And I don't say no to him. Now, why did he have to do that? It feels so good, his body heat surrounding me, his smell so familiar and comforting. My cheek brushes his neck and just that touch, it's enough to make my knees rattle.

"Do you want to sit in my truck and talk for a few more minutes?" he asks.

10:00 P.M.

Boom, we are in the cab of his truck, and our lips snap together like magnets. I take a deep breath of him, and he responds by wrapping his strong arms around me again. Oh Lordy. His hands stroke my shoulders, and something between a sigh and a laugh comes out of me. I can see his eyes in the dim light. He's drinking me in like a man who just came out of the desert.

This is one of those moments when I feel like I could easily cross the line. My whole being heats up and wants to surrender to him. He has no qualms about sex before marriage either, so it's entirely on me to hold this line. I'm trying to hold back the tide, but the waves keep coming.

10:57 P.M.

"I have to go," I finally muster the strength.

He sighs, leans back in his seat, still breathless, still looking at me with fire in his eyes. "I know," he says in a way that makes him seem defeated.

After an hour in the truck making out like teenagers, I can't even tell you how I got here. How can I be numb and over stimulated at the same time? Hypnosis. He definitely hypnotized me.

11:23 P.M.

The warm drops of water from the shower beating on my back help snap me out of it. The tingles of his touch still linger on me, the words, the food, the music. Still, my thoughts are cloudy. Logic and reason just left my body.

As I lie in bed holding my jacket with his scent, I'm left wondering what will happen next...

CHAPTER TEN

FRIDAY

12:05 A.M.

The screen on my phone lights up my otherwise dark room.

> Charm: I'm so glad you said yes to my invite tonight. I look forward to talking to you tomorrow. Good night, Beautiful.

I don't respond. I just have no idea what to say.

7:08 A.M.

I stare at the words on the phone. Nope, wasn't a dream. We went out. And everything was magical.

> Me: Me too. Good morning, how is your day going?

When I don't get a response, I get up and start moving. Time to get up, get a quick workout in.

7:33 A.M.
I'm sweaty after doing HIIT in my living room. I'll just sit down real quick and check Facebook. I realize I have not talked to Stay Woke in two days. The post of her and her beautiful daughter makes me smile. She's such a good mom. I wonder what Dreamer's been up to? Scrolling through Dreamer's feed is like reading a great self-help book. She always has the best quotes and links.

7:58 A.M.
Dang, I really need to get off this. One more person, just want to see his face. Four days ago, I deleted every sign of him off my phone, but I stopped short of unfriending him.

His face pops up on my screen. My heart does a double take, and my stomach doesn't like it. I scroll down.

He just posted two photos, one at 7:09 and the second just now at 7:51 a.m. He's in a coffee shop with a woman. I recognize her — the co-worker he dated while we were still friends. 7:09, huh? That's awfully early to meet for work. Am I jumping to conclusions, or did he give her a booty call right after he left me?

He must think I'm stupid. My face feels hot. I'm suddenly sweating. Oh right, I just worked out. I close my computer and check my phone texts just to make sure I didn't imagine it. I didn't.

10:10 A.M.
The day creeps by. My workload isn't keeping me distracted enough from the fact he was drinking coffee with that woman when I texted him, and he didn't answer.

Are we playing this game again?

I'm angrily stuffing 500 envelopes and get a paper cut. Great, right on my scrolling thumb. The cut throbs so much it surprises me.

A line of blood forms. For a second, I can feel my heart beat in my thumb.

During my break, I need to get my mind right so I go for a walk. *This is disappointing, but Candace, check yourself.* It could have been an early work meeting. Really, really early. But if he was so busy, why was he posting that meeting to his personal page?

The thing that throws me is how obvious he's being about it.

If I fly off the handle, I prove him right. This is silly. I'm an adult. I will give him the benefit of the doubt. I will be calm, but I will be direct. I'm just going to call him and clear this up.

Voicemail. Of course. More silence.

I trudge back to work feeling disheartened. Why would he do all this work to get me back in his life if he was up to something else?

My head swirls with confusion and doubt. We spent the whole dinner reaffirming that we were friends, and then I had to go and get in his truck. So which program are we going with here now?

1:15 P.M.

I'm trying to eat a sandwich with zero appetite when I finally hear from Charm.

> Him: Hey you! I got really busy at work.

Hey you? I had to double check and make sure it was from him. How about, "Sorry I missed your call," or I've got one better, "Super busy, can I call you later?"

Let me calm down. Again. Just because my workday isn't busy doesn't mean he is not. I'm reading into this. During our conversation, he mentioned when something I don't like happens, I tend to take a negative approach and that I assume the worst and react prematurely.

Me: Hey.

Oh the fury of question marks I want to fire off right now. Should I ask him if that was a work meeting he posted at 7 a.m.? Do I tell him again that I'm confused with the pledging of friendship followed by the making out?

I do not say anything. Just put my uneaten sandwich in the fridge and go back to work.

6:17 P.M.

Him: WYD

I'm in the grocery store shopping, which feels like a mighty victory considering my appetite has vacated the premises. But I'm determined to get chicken and rice and cook it and eat it if it kills me.

Me: Nothing, wyd

Him: Nothing, just got in the house about 30 mins ago.

This is agonizing, having too much to say and saying nothing. Is he going to call? This is exhausting.

7:22 p.m.

I've eaten, thank God. Did some writing. Looked mostly like this:
WTH? Am I insane or is he?
List of Things to Do When I am Over Charm....
IS THIS WHAT LOVE IS SUPPOSED TO LOOK LIKE???
I avoided my girls' phone calls. And still no call from Charm. Wow. This is not shaping up how I thought it was going to be.

8:05 PM

    Him: you ok?

    Me: Just finished up some writing ... I'm good.

This confirms that he knows I'm not okay. I want to ask him about this woman. I know there's something going on there. But I'm also confused where we left this whole thing. I was all grownup earlier today by calling him. Why am I having trouble now?

Suddenly, I have a solution to my immediate problem: Bake something worthy of posting on social media. Bingo. There's a recipe for an apple cake online. Measuring, stirring, paying attention: perfect. I pull out all the stuff I need, put some music on. Charlie walks into the kitchen to see what I'm doing, and then promptly walks back out.

I'm busy now. But I keep looking at my phone.

8:24 P.M.

I'm up to my elbows in peeled apples and flour, and he still hasn't called. This is how it always feels — he uses text to keep his distance. He's testing the fence because he wants something.

This is it, the Feeling. This is why Stay Woke wants me to Stay Away. All this mental tap-dancing trying to figure out what he's thinking. As long as he's playing the tune, I get to keep dancing.

I'm not even mad. Okay, yes I am. But not at him. I'm mad it took me this long to really understand. The lack of communication, the defensiveness, the sweet-talking, it just doesn't work for me. It never did. I gave it my all. I did my best. And maybe this is his ALL. Maybe this truly is his best.

I can't keep putting myself through this, I think to myself as I slide the dessert in the oven. It's been years now that I have waited for his actions to match his words. And maybe one day they will, but in the meantime, I'm a complete wreck. This has gone on for too long. I've never felt so embarrassed. This whole thing is *embarrassing*. Maybe shame is what I need to help me move on.

I start cleaning the kitchen. It feels good to be productive. A few versions of me argue in my head as I clean.

Candace 1: Give it some time. It's not that serious, Candace.

Candace 2: It is! It is that serious! It is entirely too soon for him to be acting like this. We don't even have 48 hours under our belt, and he's back to the same ol' mess. You lost all your seniority when you checked out, AGAIN!

Candace 3: Maybe he wouldn't be acting like this if YOU DIDN'T MAKE OUT WITH HIM …

Candace 1 and Candace 2: Oh my god, you did not just say that.

Candace 3: Well, it's true. You gave him the signal that all this nonsense is okay!

Candace 2: Nope, I'm not buying it! He's acting this way because he wants to. Why do I always act like it's my fault? If me making out with him brought this out of him, best I know now than later!

Candace 1: Maybe he's having plumbing problems? Maybe we should drive by his house real quick?

Candace 1, 2, & 3: Are you OUT OF YOUR DAMN MIND?

- This is probably why men accuse women of being crazy.

One time, a long time ago, Dreamer was dating this jerk — we'll just call him Placeholder — right after her now-husband cheated on her. And she went kinda crazy.

Placeholder managed to hold a big place with Dreamer because I sat on the phone with her many nights listening to her describe the drama. I'd listen and let her go on and on, never saying that Mr. Dreamer was the guy she needed to be dealing with. Yes, he blew it big-time, but he knew he messed up and was doing everything right to try and make amends. Placeholder, on the other hand, well, I don't need to explain.

Anyway, Dreamer one night gets super suspicious that Placeholder is holding someone else's place, if you know what I mean.

"I'm going to go over there." She sounded like she hadn't slept in a while.

"That's not a good idea."

"I just know he's up to something. Will you go with me?"

"Heck no. Are you nuts?"

"I'm coming over."

"No you don't —" she hung up.

And there I was sitting in her car in the dark, staking out his house like narcs. I had a strange craving for donuts.

"Is that light on? That's his car." She looked paranoid.

"Yeah, I think we can safely deduce that he is in his residence." Dreamer ignored me. I swear she was about to pull some binoculars out of her purse. I remember sitting there and thinking, *This idiot is not worth it. There's a guy out there who will love you and be every answer to every prayer you have ever whispered.*

She was not ready to hear that. She was getting all "X-Files" about this guy whose name would be lost to history in a matter of months. We are sitting there when Placeholder predictably walks some chick to her car and plants a kiss on her lips.

There it was, Dreamer's biggest fear materializing right before her eyes — again. She started balling. "Is this my fate?" she yelled.

Dreamer didn't date for some time after that. She poured herself into her work, which turned out to be a good use of her energy. She always says that during that time she did a lot of self-discovery. Mr. Dreamer gave her space but continued to put in the time. When she finally told me she had taken him back, I wasn't surprised. "He knows how I like my eggs," she shrugged.

9:13 P.M.

Ding! The apple cake is ready! It smells amazing! I put on the oven mitts, open the oven door and…

Come on. I pull out the best smelling, ugliest cake you will never see on social media. So much for that part. It cools on the counter while I get into pajamas. I cut a big piece and taste it. Oh man that's good.

I flip on the TV, but I'm all about this cake.

Typically, Charm waits a few months before he shows his behind like this. Now, it's like he doesn't even care. This is deliberate and the message is: Take me as I am, or be penalized with another stonewalling. Somehow the silences became a form of punishment, a threat.

Charm appears on the TV in black and white dressed like a '40s gangster: I'll give you some time alone, see, so you'll miss me enough to take me back.

Now there's me in a '40s dress with a string of pearls. I'm tied to railroad tracks: Oh no, please, I'll do anything, just don't leave me here!

Charm, (waving his pistol around): Anything, huh? Like keep your trap shut when I post pictures of other dames on the internet?

Me, (hesitating): Um…

Charm: Make up your mind, ya needy broad!

Me (seeing the train coming): Oh alright, but I don't have to like it!

Charm: Oh you'll like it, alright. Now I don't actually have to make good on any of those promises, that's how the grift works.

This is my second slice of ugly apple cake. The con was simple, actually. He wasn't making amends because he cared. It was all snake oil.

10:21 P.M.

That's it, I'm about to drop. I'm sure this whole problem will still be here tomorrow.

CHAPTER ELEVEN

SATURDAY

8:10 A.M.

The sun is shining. I'm lying in bed. Charlie hops up, and I usually don't let him, but today I do. He curls up next to me. It's Day 10. Okay technically, it's Day 11, but I don't count that Friday that disappeared.

This was supposed to be my self-imposed day of liberation. The deadline has passed.

I don't feel different. I don't feel free. In fact, I'm questioning everything even more: my desires, my needs, my relationships — even my friendships. For the last two days, I've been dodging the people who love me the most to entertain someone who won't even pick up their phone.

And for what? The sake of my own pride?

I'm writing a blue streak in my journal when Charlie squawks the "I have to pee" sound.

Okay, Buddy.

It's early, I'm in my sweats and hoodie with the hood up to hide the fact that I have done nothing to my hair. The air outside is cold enough that I can see my breath.

This is hopeless. I've spent enough time worrying about this guy who is not worrying about me. His mouth said "friendship" but that was a rouse. I wonder if that early morning post from the cafe was intentional.

We circle through the RiverWalk so that Charlie can smell some other dogs' butts. What, it's Saturday, he deserves a treat and that's his favorite activity. There are already a lot of people out, but I'm too preoccupied to care about my disheveled appearance.

I see an old couple walking an old dog. They are moving slowly, talking. They smile as we pass each other.

Why does it have to be this way? Why can't he just be a man of his word?

10:11 A.M.

I don't knock, just walk right in, knowing the door will be open. The smell of banana bread is like a hand that reaches out and draws me into the house. Already I can hear the sound of kids playing, grownups talking, pans clattering.

I come into the kitchen, where everyone always converges.

"Candace!"

"Yay!"

"Well, what a surprise!"

My mom straightens up, obviously looking for something in the fridge, and her pale face flushes with excitement at seeing me. "Hi honey!" The matriarch of my family, a white lady school teacher who adopted me along with seven other children, straightens her cardigan and gives me a warm, powerful hug. "I got that tea you like, you want a cup?"

My sister Lauren's kids zip in circles around us as she gives me a kiss on the cheek and compliments my shoes. Family. I feel better already.

"Mom told me about the story getting published, I'm so proud of you!"

"Aw, thank you."

"Did Charm take you out to celebrate?" Oh boy.

"Yes, he did," I answer, realizing I don't really have to lie since my family is totally out of the loop on these last 10 days of mayhem. But, of course, the women in my family are telepathic, and they can tell from my expression something is up.

"I wish I could stay, but I have to get the girls to dance class." Lauren can tell I need some mom time.

11:45 A.M.

"What's on your mind, Candace?"

We are settled in at the breakfast nook, steaming tea in hand, the house empty now. The birds are singing outside, and I feel the soft sunshine filtering in through mom's curtains. Everywhere you look in this house there is kids' art, and books, and crafting materials. My mom can pull a broken chair out of a dumpster, repaint it, reupholster it and make it look like she bought it out of a catalog.

I look up at my mom, the inspiration for my first piece of published writing, and I tell her everything: the breakup last Wednesday via text when we were supposed to be at Bible Study, Stay Woke and Dreamer arguing on my shoulders, undereating, overshopping, going on that fun-but-sad date with Starbucks, the acceptance letter, the weird post on Facebook at 7 a.m., and of course, my confusion after going to dinner with Charm after a week of agony.

She nods, and listens, wincing sometimes at the things Charm did, gasping with delight at my good news.

"Don't be too hard on yourself," my mom pats my arm. "You have a big heart, and sometimes it takes a few tries before big-hearted people understand — we aren't always going to get back what we put in." She takes a sip of her tea, and for a moment I feel like I climbed the mountain and am talking to a sage. Then she pops some banana bread in her mouth and gives a grunt of satisfaction. Dang it, why can't I seem to inherit the perfection of my mom's baking?

"Mom," I ask, feeling really embarrassed. "Do you like Charm? Like, actually like him?"

"Well," she pouts her lips for a moment and thinks. "I see why you like him: He's smart, energetic, he seems like he has good life goals. But I see some other things too. From what you've told me, he is hot-cold, and he acts out in ways that hurts you. I also know that around me, he's on his best behavior. Moms have a way of picking up on that."

I suddenly had a huge wave of guilt about the way Charm acted around my Mom. He was always nice to her, I mean really nice, but when we argued, he always used my mom as a weapon against me: "You have a white mom, you had it easy."

She's right, of course.

I told her I worried about the feeling that he was in my head all the time. How was I going to get rid of that?

"Oh that," she says, like I'm talking about a stain. "It fades. With time, of course." So there goes my ten days theory.

"You know," and I can see she's winding up for a big pitch, "when your father died, and I had all these children to take care of, and no one to help me, I thought there was no way I could make it without him." I give her hand a squeeze. I remember that time well. My dad was the main breadwinner, and when he died suddenly, my mom went to work full-time at the elementary school, where she still teaches. It was hard for us, and to this day, I don't know how my mom did it.

"I heard his voice in my head pretty loud sometimes, usually about things he would disapprove of. But in his absence, I learned to tell myself, no, he's not here now. This is not his choice to make, it's mine. And soon, his voice got quieter and quieter."

12:22 P.M.

After a massive lunch and another huge hug, I wander into my old room I shared with my sisters. My little corner is still neat and tidy. There are some kids books, and I'm surprised to see a journal of mine. I thought I took all of them.

"I found that in the garage the other day," Mom winks. She walks down the hall toward the family room.

I crack it open.

"My Adventure," says little me in chicken scratch handwriting. "One day, I will take a long trip." There is a crude drawing of me on a boat, I guess I'm on a cruise. "When I am growed, I will go to Europe because that is where Paris is." Tiny Candace has a suitcase and tiara on her head. "When I visit the Eiffel Tower," oh look, I even spelled it right, "I will meet a man." I flip the page. There is the cartoon me standing under the tower in what looks like a ball gown. "He will actually be a prince, but he doesn't tell me that because he doesn't want me to fall in love with him just for being a prince." I drew a man on one knee holding up a box with a giant ring in it. "Kiss him," I tell the cartoon me in the book, "then you'll see he's actually a toad."

Well, so much for childhood daydreams. I walk out of my mom's house with a chunk of banana bread wrapped in foil.

"Thanks, Mom," I wave.

"Anytime, honey," she waves back.

4:26 P.M.

I get a meme from him. It's so dumb, I immediately forget it.

Just what does he think he is doing?

8:17 P.M.

Him: We need to talk.

Except I don't have anything left to say. It's like this whole time I've been watching a stone sink to the bottom of a lake, and it finally just settled. What I want, Charm doesn't have to give.

I don't respond.

8:34 P.M.

> Him: I know what that means. No need to talk. Just when I thought things were going well, now you act like this. Regardless of my feelings, I think some things are too valuable to just throw away. I don't know what you want from me, Candace. Obviously, I'm not what you want.

My old self, my ten days ago self, would have huffed: Is he serious? Wow! So, all of it is on me? Huh! This is so typical of him. But a strange calm comes over me. It's almost, well, peaceful.

That's it, then. It's so predictable that the villain plays the victim all too well. He's wrong. He's just wrong.

I really gave this my all. I believed we could do great things together. Even after all of this, I tried one more time to see if he had it in him.

The city outside is lit up against the night sky. I'm sitting in a big comfy chair, just observing the view.

I'm glad I went to dinner with him. I got one more opportunity to see all the things I love about him. We had quite the rapport. There is still a part of me that is reaching out for all that good stuff we had going. But any story I tell myself now would mean putting my well-being aside. In every decision, thought, worry, accomplishment, up or down, he is at the forefront of my mind. I wasn't even remotely close to being on the forefront of his. Will I ever get my mind back? Then I think about what my mom said.

Nonsense. This is my brain. My heart. I am in charge of all this.

Things are going to change because from here on out I will take responsibility for me. It's easy to see how others played a part in this. Shoot, I can tell you what he did, his mom did, the devil did, I could go on. My problem is figuring out what *I did*.

And I'm going to take some time to determine that. Practically two years of my life went down the drain. But learning what part I played in this whole thing will bring me satisfaction. I don't want the time invested to be a total waste. No, I can't get the time back, but something good has got to come out of this.

It's been ten days, and to be honest, it's day 1 again. I feel confident, determined and DONE, but I was all these things ten days ago. It feels different this time, but how can I be sure?

11:55 P.M.

I drift off, but for some reason, I awake. I reach over, turn on my light, and pick up my glasses and my phone from the nightstand. No calls. I'm about to put everything away and turn the light off when something tells me to check Facebook.

And here, Dear Reader, is the final nail in the coffin. The moment I get online, someone tags Charm in a livestream at a garish, unfamiliar mansion probably near his frat house downtown. The camera is swinging, and there is loud, thumping music and bodies everywhere. Charm emerges on the screen, and he is clearly blotto. His clown drunk bros embarrass themselves in the background. Or they would be embarrassing themselves, if they had any shame.

Next, I see Charm taking shots with a Ms. Look-at-Me, a different one this time. The camera swings, and I see another woman with three men circled around her and grinding on her.

Pardon me while I dry heave over the edge of the bed. Whoo. Okay. I'm back. Let me finish my investigating.

I'm no expert, but I'd say Charm and Ms. Look-at-Me are doing tequila shots because the woman has a lime in her long pointy claws, and Charm is licking salt off her cleavage. The camera swings back again, and now I'm looking at a dusty white coffee table. Maybe the maid had the day off.

I look at the clock, four minutes to midnight.

I turn the phone off, set it aside and turn the light back off.

No doubt I'm revolted. I feel like I just drank a whole bottle of hot sauce. It's that same moment Dreamer had on the stakeout. It's the worst feeling, and yet …

The burning subsides. Any fire I had left in my heart for that man just got doused. This is scorched earth, that's what this is. There's nothing left.

I feel myself let go of the rope. Really, truly, let go.

Something opens up in me, I can't explain it, but I'm lighter — like smoke or mist. I'm sad but more than that, *I'm done.* That wasn't an accident, that impulse to look. That livestream came on right as I opened the app. It was God, showing me the truth. Charm wanted me to see him out there acting a fool, and my heart felt the tip of that knife the moment he took the jab.

God might as well have just tapped me on the shoulder, and said, "Candace, check Facebook."

Sitting up, I see my reflection in the mirror, even in the dark. Suddenly, it feels important to take a good look at myself, so I do, standing barefoot in front of the full length in my nightie.

Looking past my shape, past my hair and skin, right into my eyes. I want the woman in the mirror to talk back to me. She's smarter, this

Present Woman Who Is Me. She isn't the Me I Hoped to Be, but she is reality ... I tightly close my eyes and exhale.

Would my ten days have looked different if I had "this" me to help me through it ... I open my eyes for another look, and say out loud ...

PART 2

It's alright, Candace. It's me. I mean, you. I'm your intuition, your Present Self. I can see your eyes full of questions. Well hopefully, I can answer them.

See, I've been here all along. This rejection feels really familiar, doesn't it? Like when Dad died. That deep sense of abandonment that doesn't quite make sense. The feeling of being cut loose from something that you don't think you can live without.

I was there when you lost your way. Life handed you a raw deal. I was also there when you promised you'd never get close enough to get hurt again. And then you did. I'm proud of you for that. I watched you reopen your heart to the possibility that maybe, just maybe, you'd finally get your Happily Ever After.

Maybe I wasn't insistent enough, or maybe this whole "good boundaries" thing just takes time. I was there trying to keep your feet on the ground when he swept you off of them, and I was there after each disappointment.

I wanted to say something. But how could I? You had your agenda and wouldn't listen to me. You weren't ready, you had more tears and sleepless nights to encounter. All I could do was pray for your heart's safety and wait for the day to come.

Well, here it is. I think you are ready to hear me now.

I'm not trying to be unkind, Candace. Just the opposite.

I can see that you are a little afraid. Like the dream is over. Like every fresh disappointment will only lower your standards. I hate that it took all of this to get to this place. But Girl, you are right where you need to be.

Let's really put this time to use. Let's look at this whole thing again. Let's start on Day 1.

DAY ONE
———

FORGIVENESS PHASE 1

Swish. Imagine you are like Peter Pan and you can fly. You are an eagle circling back over two Wednesdays ago. This time, with a bird's eye view.

Before we get to the Forgiveness part, we have to Acknowledge some things.

See you down there, barely awake reading that text, on the day of Bible Study, your most sacred weekly ritual. That text was a wrecking ball on your whole world. Well here I am, Your Present Self saying to you: Your response was understandable, but you were also "in it," just too busy being hurt and confused. Looking at it from up here, the signal in that text (and all the signals before that) was clear as a bell: He didn't value the connection enough to fight for it. He just didn't have the tools.

Things you did right that day:
- Went to work
- Called your friends
- Had a good cry

Things you should have done:
- Gone to Bible Study!

He wouldn't have shown up. And hearing the word of God and studying with your church family would've made the rest of the week a whole lot easier. You let him scare you away from your place of refuge. Never let anyone do that again.

First, forgive yourself, like Mom said. You saw a wounded but awesome person underneath all that front. His story hooked you.

Remember the time the two of you went to the carnival and a guy attempted to cut? How angry Charm got? During the car ride home, he recalled when his little brother's bike got stolen when they were kids and how they were afraid to go home to deliver the news. Their father whooped them for what seemed like hours when he found out. Their mother was too afraid to intervene. Who could blame her? She had been his punching bag for years.

When Charm's father went to jail on a drug charge, Charm thought that was God's way of saving his family. They were all finally free from the abuse his father inflicted, but then his mom raised Charm and his siblings on her own.

You saw how determined he was to overcome those abusive patterns — he would never hurt a woman the way his father hurt his mother. But the trauma of his father's actions did affect him. How would he know how to treat you well with no example of what that looks like?

So his struggle, his story, were both endearing and admirable, and yet he used it like a tool. He played that angle all the way with you.

You were with him constantly, and he gave you this sense that you knew a version of him that no one else did. You knew the guy who whisked you away to Santa Monica and planned a picnic on the beach after realizing he mistook your birthday for the wrong the weekend. You knew the guy who sent roses to your job every day for two weeks with a card that read "I messed up." The guy that made watching a movie on the sofa a major production with popcorn, candy and slushies.

You can't say, "You wouldn't understand," because I do. I get the back and forth once you got used to his touch, scent, energy. But do you know how many women end up in toxic relationships and say to their girlfriends and families, "You wouldn't understand, you don't know him like I do?"

We women ignore the red flags. They were there, flapping during the late night conversations and the sharing of secrets. You extended him credit because he let you in on those secrets. It's part of the hustle.

So when you heard he was a flirt and saw him being extra friendly with ladies on social media, you justified it, extending more credit. When he told you he couldn't keep a relationship and acted like he didn't know why, more credit.

It's important to acknowledge that he did a number on your mental health, and he did it — how do I want to say this — reflexively. You were enrolled and you made more excuses for him than he made for himself. He didn't have to have a pity party or feel bad about his upbringing because you took on that responsibility. Because of his hard life, you didn't hold him to a standard of respect.

Again, don't be too hard on yourself, Candace. You wanted to help him heal, and that is admirable. But if you pick up a shard of glass, it'll cut you. Instead of being mindful of how to handle a sharp and dangerous object, you picked it up without protection. Now you're left bleeding.

He didn't treat you like a queen, as you deserved, so you couldn't treat him like the king you thought he was. First, he would have to see himself as a king worthy of a queen, and he never did.

And look, those flags were attractive. They were a challenge, and he gave you every signal that you were the woman to address them. Think about your first impression upon meeting him: You felt trouble. Your body screamed "uh oh." So why even put a guy like that in the "friend zone?" How could you identify that he was trouble, and still think he would make a good friend?

Confidence is good will toward yourself. Arrogance is rooted in deep insecurity, a real need to prove yourself. These are easy things to mischaracterize.

So why did you ignore the warning signs that God was showing you and everyone else pointed out? Those warning signs:

- Abuse in his background (more specifically, his attitude toward it)
- Radio silence
- Side hustle dealing weed (oh you thought I was going to skip over that, didn't you?)
- His temper
- Jealousy
- Other women

You clearly saw these warning signs but decided they weren't that bad.

And here's another Acknowledgement: Many times you over spiritualized wrongdoings as an excuse to buy yourself more time. "Let me just pray on my next move. Let me seek God and see what I should do. Charm's making headway, right?"

Be truthful. That man acted like a complete clown, and you didn't need to consult God on whether to leave the circus or not. Marriage would've been a completely different carnival; as the girlfriend, you can still walk.

Look down again as you drive to work and sob in the Jeep. He tore you down because you didn't think objectively. And hey, you were cautious in the beginning, so give yourself credit for that. You just didn't remain objective.

Flaws are flaws. All humans have them. It was and is okay that he had a horrible childhood, and he had to hustle to survive. It makes sense he doesn't manage his emotions well.

But this man zapped you with his romantic stun gun, rocked you way off balance, made you contort into a woman you didn't recognize. That's unacceptable.

And now, here we are.

Day 1 sucks, no lie. The pain you feel is awful. But look at you down there in bed wrestling with the idea that somehow you could've done something different and then you would still be with Charm. That's how well that romantic stun gun works.

All right. We're done counting red flags. All isn't lost. Come here, let's hug it out.

DAY TWO

LOYALTY, DREAMS AND WOKE REALITY

Here you are on Day 2, a hot mess still in pajamas at noon. Your friends are sweet and are trying to give you good advice. Dreamer just wants you to be happy, and that's forgivable, but this message that *you* did something wrong, uh-uh. You didn't. So funny that the idealist, the romantic in this pageant was the little devil sitting on your shoulder.

Dreamer came around to Stay Woke's side when she saw behind Charm's curtain. And more than that, your friends reflect each side of your personality. Dreamer is the part of you that really wants love and romance. Nothing wrong with that. But that's why we have Stay Woke.

This girl has her eyes open. Next time you see her, remember to tell her that. I'll remind you.

Another memory just jumped in, about loyalty, Dreams and Woke Reality.

It was movie night, one of our most fun rituals where we get junk food, relax in loungewear and watch a chick flick. We were at Stay Woke's house (it surprises me she's just as much of a sucker for a good rom-com as anybody), indulging in popcorn and deciding what to watch. She was thumbing through the classics we'd seen dozens of times.

"Alright, here we go: 'The Notebook?' "

"Aw, that one is so sweet."

"Yeah, but we watch that one the most."

" 'Pretty Woman?' "

"Played out, although it's worth watching the whole thing just for the necklace scene."

"True. 'Titanic?' "

All of us burst into song: "And I know that my HEART WILL GO OOOON!!" We all fell out laughing, holding our sides. We finally decided on *"Runaway Bride."* Richard Gere and Julia Roberts — the gold standard in on-screen chemistry.

The movie tells the story of Maggie (Roberts) who stood up three guys at the altar, which earned her some unwanted media attention and the nickname "Runaway Bride." Graham (Gere), is a cynical journalist who doesn't think highly of the opposite sex. He sees an opportunity and decides to visit Maggie's hometown and write a story on her, with the hope it will give his career a boost. Maggie, a spirited can-do kind of gal, is engaged for the fourth time, and Graham is convinced she will flee. He wants to be right there when it happens so he can get the scoop.

Of course, what he isn't prepared for is Maggie's charm, and the realization that all the men in her past had no idea who she was. Maggie was a trophy for those men, and so at the last moment, she would bail.

As he is interviewing Maggie's family, neighbors and the three dumped grooms, Graham would always ask the question: "How does she like her eggs?" To which they each replied, "same as me." It becomes clear that Maggie changed her tastes: fried, scrambled, over easy, etc. to suit the guy she was with at the time, partly because none of them ever asked her.

That theme got us talking, more like shouting, specifically Dreamer. "Why do women do that? We find someone, and once we connect ourselves to that person, we totally disconnect from ourselves?"

"Well that's obvious," Stay Woke replies. "That's what we've been taught to do for centuries. 'Please our man.' For most of history, women have been subjugated to men." Hard to argue, but dang I hate that word "subjugate."

"There is a fine line between compromising in a healthy way, and bending over backwards for someone who doesn't deserve it," says me, the woman who would write a book about how she bent over backwards for someone who didn't deserve it.

"It's as if we've convinced ourselves that it's better to be exactly like them than to be 100% ourselves," Dreamer preached. Stay Woke gave a "hallelujah hand wave" as a sign of encouragement.

Well you can guess how the movie ends: After doing all this research (that we would now refer to as "stalking"), Graham sees that Maggie is not some kind of hysterical joke, but an incredible person and he out-alphas the groom. Finally, Maggie gets to have her wedding cake and eat it too. She gets to be in love *and* be herself.

I think back to that night and the words Dreamer spoke and how they resonate even more now than they did then. I picked up habits and hobbies just to appease him.

I traded my identity just as Maggie did, all for the sake of being able to say I have "someone." And now I'm here. How ironic too, that after all the accommodating I did, he still did what he wanted and left me looking stupid.

Mr. Dreamer made one slip and that was in high school, Reader. We can forgive him for being young and dense, right? He has been a loyal, loving, committed husband and dad ever since. What Dreamer did — find a man who cared enough to figure out how she liked her eggs — was the best decision she ever made. It led her back to the one who she's now yoked with. No pun intended. Okay, I totally intended.

So there's actually two kinds of loyalty we are talking about here: our loyalty to our own identities as women in love and loyalty to other people.

For us to be loyal to ourselves, I'm realizing, takes practice. Charm used to accuse me of being spoiled all the time. Mostly because my mom is white. But really, he was just breaking down my sense of self, my preferences and the parts of my personality that were difficult for him. I didn't stick up for myself. I let him chip away at me.

But now that I see that, I know what the opposite looks like, the guy who knows how I like my eggs. That man will know how to stand in his truth and still be cool with me standing in mine.

Loyalty must be earned, and the way people— men, women, friends, neighbors, co-workers, etc.— demonstrate they are worthy is by backing up what they say with action.

DAY THREE

BARGAINING

Technically, this day completely disappeared, so we are going to use it to further analyze Day 2. Yes Candace, Day 2 took two days.

Today, you did some 21st century stalking. Yep, stalking. So simple these days, no stakeouts necessary. Besides, who has the gas for that? Now you can stalk your ex-boyfriend from the comfort of your own home! With the click of a button, and the flick of a thumb, it's never been easier to obsess!

You reread his wack text messages over and over again as though trying to crack a code. You knew them by heart so you could repeat them to yourself throughout the day. Here was your journal entry that day: "I feel like crap, Day 3 sucks, here we go again."

It's just like the stages of grief when someone dies. There is a cycle. This phase is called Bargaining.

The ego resists the idea that he was choosing something else. Which is partly true, but there's more to it than that. Regardless of his agency over his own choices, there is part of you that rebels against the slap of rejection.

Your pride wants to know why! Your pride says, how could you not choose me? Who are you to be the one to change the dynamics of our relationship? Sometimes it's our love for the person, but sometimes, it's our pride wanting answers to our questions. It makes no sense because whatever response we get, it won't satisfy us one bit. That's the human heart for you.

But I get it, when a person has given us promises of a future or insisted that we hold out for commitment, it can be devastating when they have a change in heart. But that's the risk of love. Where there's no risk, there's no reward.

Strategies to use instead of trolling the dude on the net:
- Take a bath
- Give the dog a bath (not at the same time)
- Go to a midday movie rather than binge on your couch
- Eat something healthy
- Try a new activity

Today would have been a good day to block him from your phone and delete him from your life. Get him off your social media. Just take away the temptation. Why would you give someone who doesn't want to be in your life a peek inside it? He doesn't get to know what we've got going on. He lost that right. It's not like seeing his status and pictures make you feel any better. Look at you, you actually feel worse. Every time you log on and see that he's alive and well and choosing not to communicate with you, it hurts. Powering down would have been a smart move.

DAY FOUR

GOOD DISTRACTIONS

You did okay with this day. You got out of the house. You met with your people at church. You did some harmless escapist techniques, and there is room for that. These things take time. You just don't want it to become a habit.

I probably said this already, but it bears repeating: When you are feeling blue, use the trick Mom taught you — focus on someone else. When she was younger, and she had a really bad day, she would find someone to help. Even the simplest thing, like helping someone cross the street, is a way to come outside of yourself. And it feels good to help.

DAY FIVE

BAD DISTRACTIONS

This day started off so strong, girl. You went to church, and it was such a relief to be there. That was another solid move. But while we are on the topic of God, full disclosure…

It's hard to tell sometimes what God wants for us. You thought you got some pretty clear signs that Charm was the Prince Charming you were looking for, right? Mmm, no, not really. Those were more like shiny distractions on the surface of the water that prevented you from seeing what was lurking underneath.

The real signs were the observations, the friction and the intense instability you felt when he disappeared.

Prayer is necessary, but what was the content of that prayer, Candace? Were you asking for help? Were you begging for Charm to grow up and fully realize you? Maybe next time, you'll ask for clear eyes.

And what about community help? Any struggle at all should have support. There are leaders at the church who've seen it all. They have wise and helpful things to say. Listen to them!

All right, fast-forward to the evening. Let's take a look at this Starbucks fiasco.

The ego, again. Sigh. How sneaky it is! When a person gets dumped, that person feels ugly, rejected, unwanted. The easiest thing in the world is to find a new, eager reflection of yourself.

This genuine, hardworking man who loves God — he reaches out, and you don't bat an eye. Was that honest about your situation? No. And by not being honest, you didn't give him a choice. You could have said, "Listen, I was seeing someone, it didn't work out. I'm in no shape for anything serious at the moment, but I really enjoy your company and if you'd still like to spend some time together, I'm down."

Then Starbucks could have made his own choice, with all the facts in front of him.

Instead, Candace, *you sought outer validation.* Your needing to feel better about yourself had NOTHING to do with Starbucks, the poor dude. Here is where Dreamer switched shoulders to the angel side. He was in it for the right reasons, to find a mate, and you hired him for the evening to feel better about yourself. And he showed you a great time! It was like picking up right where you two left off.

The other side of that coin is that you wanted to prove something to Charm.

You went out with Starbucks and had a phenomenal time. But it wasn't real, you even knew it at the time. It's alright, God made sure you got the message.

This is the message: Starbucks himself might not be right for you, *but men like him exist.* It is a woman's dream to marry into a great family, and he had a phenomenal one. His parents have been married for about 40 years, and from what you'd heard about them, they represent true "relationship goals."

Starbucks was different from Charm in every way. He was a serious dude with a straightforward approach. He was clear that he was into you. You hate when men aren't honest about their intentions and where they are in life. You hate feeling like you wasted time with a dude who was not ready, or meant no good.

On the other hand, you could've taken this "perfect" guy for a ride; there are plenty of women out there that do. But you didn't. You knew it wasn't right. So this was a good lesson, albeit an uncomfortable one within ten big days of uncomfortable lessons: Rebounds don't work, and we shouldn't use other people's emotions to cope with our own.

When you plant seeds of honesty, they will show up for you in one way or another. You reap what you sow.

DAY SIX

GRATITUDE

Remember this day? A welcome relief from the heartbreak when you got some outer validation that you deserved? The acceptance letter! And it couldn't have come at a better time. Thanks again, God.

That sure put a smile on your face that quickly vanished because you couldn't share it with you-know-who.

Well, here's me just reminding you that when something like this happens, you need to fully own it. And while you are feeling magnanimous, turn to all the other blessings in your life and say a big warm, full-hearted *thank you*.

A breakup makes us feel small, and the loss clouds all the other wonderful things in our lives. It's easy for single people to get into this negative headspace — that life sucks because you aren't in love.

Come on now. Look at your life. You have people who love you, you have ambition, and strength and smarts. In short, you got it going on, and that doesn't change if you are with someone or not.

This acceptance was a sign that your hard work is paying off. You are making progress, and that says a lot in this uncertain world. Believe in that, Candace.

DAY SEVEN

MARSHALING

I'm labeling this day "marshaling" because it's a good example of using the resources around you in a positive way: your female friends. Women in general are a powerful source of positive energy, and we don't talk about that enough. It's your girlfriends who pick you back up after you've struck out, and they are the ones who will dust you off and pat you on the back for trying, even if you fail.

I think we can chalk this one up as another success. Sort of.

There you are with Stay Woke and Dreamer, dressed to the nines, laughing and talking and celebrating. It's important to note that Dreamer had a serious change of heart in the course of this conversation, and that both your girls recognized that this Charm fella was no good for you. And you *still* went another round with him. But we'll get to that.

You may not always agree with them, but you are lucky to have friends like Stay Woke and Dreamer, who have your back and will tell you what is up. Women are just naturally better at some things: solving problems, bouncing back from bad situations, helping other people and addressing their emotions.

And let's not forget about co-workers, not the nosey ones. I'm sure one of the nights that didn't go so well could have ended in a fun and much-needed happy hour if you went to work.

All that is a gift.

DAY EIGHT

RELAPSE/BACKSLIDING

Yeah. This was where things went off the rails. Things were going great, if memory serves. You were starting to take care of yourself and make career plans, and then he called. Instantly, you floated out in fantasyland, seeing possible explanations. In plain terms: You panicked.

I could sit you down here and lecture you about letting this unhealthy romance back in, but you know all that. We know how this story ends, and we know that you, Candace Past, became me, Candace Present, and so it all turns out well. You had to go around with him one more time just to make sure.

But I think it's worth looking at some more examples in the course of that conversation where you didn't stand in your own truth.

So to recap. Here's one instance:

"Candace, can we still be friends?"

"Yes."

You knew that was not going to work. You sat still for all that small talk. You bent to his will when he offered to take you out. I could go on. But if you were going to pick that phone up, you should have said to him: "This tug of war isn't working for me. I've told you what I want and need, even from a friendship, and you haven't been able to deliver." You get the picture.

After those agonizing eight days in the desert, to have his attention again felt like arriving at an oasis. It's similar to the feeling of an addict falling off the wagon: amazing in the moment, and horrible right after.

Now I know this is easy to say and hard to do, but again, we come back to this part about self-respect. This man didn't respect you, and we know this now because he was living this double life. On the weekends with you it was nice dinners and concerts and church, and on the weekdays, it was frat parties with hookers and drugs.

Let's zoom in, shall we? Here he is, testing the fence. But let's ask ourselves: What was he doing for those eight days?

He was enjoying his new freedom. He was at the strip club with his "brothers." He was having his cake and eating Ms. Look-at-Me too.

Oh look, there he is, flattering you, re-enrolling you in his life by referencing his nephew. Oh and there he goes, getting all excited about your story acceptance. Peep the game, Candace!

Now hold on, because I'm going to roll the tape further back. I see you groaning, but come on, we have to look at this dead in the eye.

About six months into the relationship, the actual romance, you were over at Charm's house on a weeknight. He had been acting restless, getting kind of snippy. He was drinking that night, a behavior that never pleased you.

Remember how he asked if you wanted some of his fruit punch drink, and you said yes? Yep, I can see on your face that you do. Ah here we are: He hands you a cup with red liquid and sits down in front of you, waiting for you to taste it.

It burns as only liquor can. Man, whatever that was, it stung like the Beyhive coming to Beyoncé's defense. You just spit it out and look up.

Charm is laughing at you. He did it on purpose.

"You're so uptight, Candace. Why can't you ever relax?"

Freeze. Look at your face. This was a big line in the sand he just stepped over. He knows full well that you don't consume alcohol. He wanted to bring you to his level.

Okay let's roll forward, back to the First Call in Eight Days. He's spinning the conversation to look like, somehow, this whole conflict is your fault. It's your uptightness that's the problem. See much of a difference between that and spiking a non-drinker's drink? Me neither.

Also, real talk: He kept you on the call until 1:00 a.m. Girl, isn't that, like, a cult technique? Depriving someone of their sleep?

DAY NINE

MORE RELAPSE/ ROCK BOTTOM

Here it is. The last time you saw him. Where do you think you're going? Get back here, Candace.

Ahem. Now, where was I? Oh yes. If you didn't think this day was going to be a blow-by-blow, well, sit down. Let's start with the texting. You are still trying to do that dance, keep your dignity, but be all good about your boundaries by having him meet you there instead of pick you up. Like you didn't make the huge concession of a "just friends dinner." Do you see how much energy you are spending on this guy right now as you try to figure out whether you should respond with, "hey there," or "hi?" Steam is practically coming out of your ears.

There you are, running around like a hound with its head stuck in a bucket. Alright we don't need to watch every embarrassing moment, so let's skip quickly through you looking ridiculous at the gym, getting ready like you are meeting some dignitary, and then, ah, here we are. The dinner.

Note the approach to door. You, in slow motion, looking glamorous (okay well done with the outfit, to point out some positives in this critique) as you enter Maggiano's. Credit where credit is due: You do look hot. But for all the wrong reasons.

Flip to the table talk. Him snake charming you. You carb loading. Good grief, Candace, enough with the bread.

Let's turn the volume up:

"Candace, it has really not been easy without you. I know it's only been a couple days," (I know, I know, it's been a week, but pay attention) "but it's like, all my effort in trying to get that promotion, you were there for all of that, you are the one person who knows what it means for me to get passed up." You frown here, and he checks himself. "I'm not trying to talk about myself, I just feel, and have always felt from the first time we met, that we could do great things together, and support each other."

I'll turn the sound back down here so we can discuss. He's being needy, and you are supposed to take this as a sign of your specialness. And you do. We'll skip over all the laughing, all the fawning. Up, here we go, walking back to the car. Now you're hugging, oh now you're in the truck, here comes the making out! Let's um, slow this scene down, shall we?

Oh my, well would you look at that? Oh his hand is, wait, I can't see now because the windows are fogging up…Okay, you get the picture. I'm not trying to embarrass you. Well, maybe a little. Here's my point. You had genuine animal chemistry with him, and while you could control it, he could not, and while we are talking truth, there really aren't a ton of men who hold out for marriage. Lots of them have a public "girlfriend" that they trot out to church and also a series of meaningless secret hookups on the side. For Charm, you were clearly the former.

Alright, let's get real about understanding this relapse. He had a pretty good grip on you — psychologically, spiritually and physically.

And when you break up with someone, sometimes those different parts don't all leave together. Sometimes your heart, and also in this case, your body, remains tethered. I am proud of you for standing your ground when it came to intimacy. Lord knows he did his best to get you to break that vow. And he didn't. As much as you wanted him, that is something you save for your husband.

I'm thinking of a different moment, another memory when Charm let the charm slip. It was on vacation, to the Bahamas, remember? You were in Florida for a few days first, and he was clearly frustrated with you. He kept making all kinds of noise about unimportant things, but what was really going on? He thought he was taking you on this vacation, and you were finally going to let him get some.

So he got angry. He stormed off. He left you in a strange place. Because he was not going to get laid. Even though you had made it clear that was not going to happen.

Back to this problem of him having a hold over you on a sensual level — you were never safe with him, were you? The relationship might have felt good when things were good, but how did it feel to have to reject his advances over and over again? How did it feel to have him storm off and leave you in a parking lot? Not great. And not physically safe.

I think everyone experiences this relapse principle when they fall in love with someone who isn't right for them. Bonds tend to snap back before they break.

But next time you date someone, as you are vetting and he is courting, watch to see if your body feels safe around him. All the time. There should be no exceptions to that.

You were always an object to him, a prize he had to win. That's why when he acted out, he looked down on you, because it made him feel superior. "You had it all growing up. You didn't have to fight to survive like I did," he would snarl at you. Somehow, having a white mom meant you didn't have problems. Nevermind that your dad died when you were young. Nevermind you had seven siblings and your mom had to clip coupons and keep a side hustle refurbishing old furniture on top of being a full-time teacher. His life was hard, yours was easy, as far as he was concerned.

None of that is true, and how would that have played out if you had stayed together — him always resenting you and your family because you had a strong family unit and he didn't?

DAY TEN

FORGIVENESS PHASE 2

Good thing you visited your mom on this day, got some grounding and some banana bread. Once you heard yourself explain the last nine days, going down the list, you got a chance to see how all these broken pieces looked together. And that's exactly what the relationship was: broken.

This is the day the final letdown arrives, the day he affirmed, once again, how he intended to conduct himself. All these arguments with the various parts of "Candace," they were now all speaking in the same voice: ME. There was no more mystery, or anxiety about whether or not this fool was going to get his act together. He wasn't. And then it all fell into place, didn't it? You see his true colors splashed across your screen like spilled tequila.

By the way, fun fact: That strange intuition you had around midnight that caused you to look at Facebook? That was me! Your intuition! I know, I know, it was convenient that the shit show (I'm sorry, I try not to swear, but there is simply no other word for it) on the video, with professional escorts and the rails of booger sugar on the table in the background, happened to be at that moment. All I had to do was get you to pick up your phone. And guess who else was watching in. Yep: Dreamer was sitting at her screen doing some late night work and whoa. So if she had any doubts about Charm still being your "one and only," well, that's gone like the line of coke up that joker's nose.

Do you remember what happened next? Of course you do. It's the BIG MOMENT that you loved yourself enough to let go.

You pictured your friends, who came out for you and how you ignored them so you could have this one more round with him. You saw your mom — loving, funny, powerful — and are reminded again how he tried to frame all that as a liability, rather than a strength. And the rest, they say, is history.

I am proud of you for this moment. It took strength, it took guts. It took the wisdom to know that you are worth way more than how Charm treated you. Whenever you feel down about this roller coaster you climbed on, just remember you got off the ride. This is something you can be proud of for the rest of your life.

BUT — there is one more thing, and it means coming full circle with the forgiveness piece. Yes, Candace, you know what's coming don't you?

Yep. You have to forgive Charm. Sit down. I SAID SIT DOWN. Whew. Hear me out, will you?

When I say "forgiveness," you are thinking an act, like in elementary school when the teacher made you and your classmate walk to the front of the class and say, "I'm sorry I pulled your pigtail," and then the other would say, "I'm sorry I said you can't come to my birthday party," and then the teacher made you shake, and everything was supposed to be resolved. That's what you were thinking, right?

Well this is not that. I'm in no way suggesting that you make yourself vulnerable to Charm again, no, quite the opposite. He should be avoided at all costs. This kind of forgiveness doesn't require you to make up with the person. Feel better now?

Forgiveness in this case is, like you said, letting go of the rope. It's accepting that this is where he is at right now in his life, and it's not for you, and then, gently unhooking yourself from that person. Pretty good, right? I can't take credit for that turn of phrase. I'm pretty sure that was Oprah.

Here's the tricky part: You have to accept the fact that these were Charm's choices, as nonsensical and personally tragic as they seemed. All you have to do is look at his wounds and his inflated ego, and you can see which impulses were driving that bus. There are layers to every person, some of them admirable, and some of them sad and horrifying. Charm's layers, and the way they manifested in the world, were unhealthy. Oh look at me, I'm talking like some kind of new age self-help person. My sister would be proud.

Back to forgiveness. It's layered too, right? You have to forgive yourself, and you have to release that other person, and eventually forgive them too, (although maybe not to their face). It's a humbling process, and it takes time.

This is a slight tangent, but bear with me: Even if Charm had been consistent with his messaging and behavior, and had still decided to send that breakup text, rejection is part of adulthood, and we all experience it. Also, this is America; we can change our minds all we want! We've been on both sides — you've dumped somebody and somebody has dumped you — and in both of those scenarios, you came out okay. Not only did you live, but you were glad it happened once you got some distance and saw it wasn't going to work. God always exposes why the split needed to happen.

Forgiveness is a road, some wise man said.

We can't penalize a person for their nature, and we also can't expect them to change it for us. You were looking for intimacy, Charm was looking for pleasure. Quality vs. Quantity.

And on that Saturday night when you woke up and got that impulse to check social media, where just a minute before someone posted that photo of Charm & Ms. Tequila, that was the moment of your unhooking. Thanks, in part, to me.

I want you to see that there is a difference between disconnecting and forgiving. You can never see Charm again for the rest of your life and seethe with rage forever. Or you can relinquish all the toxic feelings for him.

Here is where Jesus can help...if you let Him. You don't want to live in resentment, do you? Frankly, it takes more energy to cling to all that bitterness than it does to let it go. LET IT GO, LET IT GOOOOO!! Like Queen Elsa in "Frozen." Ahem. I'm sorry, Reader. Forgive me once again for my Disney affinity.

As I was saying. When you truly do the work, you will render Charm charmless. You won't feel strange if you bump into him or learn about his antics. You will be instead liberated from the circus. So in this moment, right before midnight, you took the first step in releasing yourself, forgiving yourself and even forgiving him. I'm not saying this is easy. But it's much easier than hating someone.

RESOLUTION/RESOLVE

Welcome back to the present, Candace. You are in the Now again. There are just a few more little goodies I want to show you. After all, you might be thinking, what about this whole love thing? It turns out this whole falling out of love thing has many, many steps to it. But I think you're going to like this part.

I want you to come to the mirror again. There we are. Yes, you just woke up, and yet, look at you! You are beautiful, talented, loving, a good friend, a hard worker, a woman of God. I want you to fully acknowledge all this without looking away. This is the difference between ego and confidence. If you are confident, because you acknowledge your own strengths and you have faith in your beliefs, none of this petty stuff matters now when you have this self-love piece in play. Think of all the losers you will now avoid after all this craziness!

And now, finally: I have a gift for you. No, it's not shoes. It's better than that. I'm going to give you a glimpse into the future. What, you don't believe that I, Your Present Self, Your Intuitive, Higher Self, can achieve that? Well, watch and learn.

Hmmm, let's see, a juicy moment from the future, so many choices, how do I pick one? Well, there's that one a few months from now, but I want that one to be a surprise. Hmm. Alright, alright! I'll pick one. Here's a good one.

Look down. This is about nine months after the Ten Day Charm Breakup Challenge. See, there's you — on stage with a panel of men and women talking about love and relationships. You look so cute in that business suit! Don't believe me? Go ahead, listen in:

"Alright now is this a deal breaker, when your girlfriend is still talking to her ex?" A couple of the men sitting on the stage raise up a "No" card.

What are you doing? You are facilitating the discussion, silly! Yeah, see after you completed this book, all this amazing stuff starts to happen. You will get both men and women in your community talking about relationships in a new way (this is not an invitation to go talking trash all over town about Charm, as tempting as that may be). No, you are talking about love at this new level. How to communicate, what you learned from that whole drama. And people started to listen.

That's right, you're giving presentations, Candace!

Okay I know what you're thinking: How am I qualified to talk to people about relationships — I'm single! Well, you are actually a poster child for someone who is sticking to her principles when it comes to relationships and marriage. Ironically, you are more desirable than ever now that you're single.

Exciting, right? Okay, I can't let you watch too much future, just a little glimpse, besides, you have work to do.

I just wanted you to see that because there is so much light at the end of this tunnel when it comes to healing yourself.

I can't give too much away here, but I can tell you this: Every wrenching pain, every tear, every sweet memory you have left over — it's all part of one thing, the narrative of your life, if you will. You can take these lemons and make lemonade, just like Beyoncé. Did I say that already?

And by the way, you don't need to worry about how you'll feel or what you'll do if you accidentally cross his path again. Trust me, you will know what to do. You won't be mad. You'll even be polite. And it won't phase you. He, on the other hand, will probably squirm.

This life experience will continue to serve you in some unexpected ways, like this book, and every conversation or presentation you have afterwards. You will continue to grow, and that is magnetic to people.

And when I say magnetic, I'm not talking just about your friends and family. I'm also talking about men. Real Men.

You see, this book, your story, it's like a bat signal. It's a beacon that's going to help you get closer to what you want in love and life. This is a net gain, money in the bank. With interest. Trust me on this.

This heartbreak, and all the writing you did to understand it, will broaden your access to people who are as ambitious and intelligent as you. And before you give up on the idea that there are men out there who share your values and want that holy kind of union, let me just assure you. They are out there, seeking, just like you.

None of this may have happened like you planned. That's life. But you have arrived, Candace. This romantic mishap polished you into a jewel. It's your time to shine.

EPILOGUE

5:15 A.M.
So it is possible to rid yourself of a toxic relationship in ten days. It was a painful process, but I did it. This is what I'm thinking when my alarm goes off. My eyes open. Today is the day: my honeymoon.

I jump out of bed, quickly get dressed, my clothes already laid out from the night before. Charlie, bless his little doggy heart, is already at my sister's house. Oh my goodness, I am going to miss his little old man face!

After some quick breakfast of instant oatmeal (I had to clear the fridge out) and a shot of coffee, I wash the dishes, brush my teeth, brush my hair, do my makeup and go over my list one more time to make sure I have everything. Like a flash, I am dressed in comfortable clothes. Then I call a car and water the plants. Good luck, green things! I'll be gone ten whole days! I power everything down and zip my suitcase.

My phone chimes my ride is here, so I roll my suitcase out, lock the front door, and take the stairs. Whoo! This thing is heavy, maybe five pairs of shoes was too much?

It's still dark outside, the street is empty. The car is at the base of the front stoop waiting. Here we go. The first phase in my adventure. I take a deep breath, and hoist my suitcase down the steps.

I approach the car, struggling down the steps with this huge rose gold bag of mine. The driver is a good-looking guy, about my age, maybe a little younger. He jumps out of the car and runs around to help get my suitcase into the trunk. "Hi Candace," he even opens the passenger door for me. I hop in, make myself comfortable. His ride is clean and smooth. I hope that's a good omen. He's even got water, fancy. I grab one and take a swig.

"Looks like you are going to DTW?"

"Yep, that's right."

"Where are you headed?"

"Paris."

"For real?!"

"Yes! I'm so excited! I barely slept last night!"

Yes, Reader, that's right. I'm taking this honeymoon by myself.

After the breakup with Charm, I realized I still had those tickets hanging over my head. I was on the phone with Stay Woke who said she might be able to finesse it with the airlines and get them to credit the Paris trip to some other ticket in the future.

And then something in me clicked, and I thought, NO.

The Disney dream of marriage and kids and happily ever after tied up neatly in a bow followed me my whole life. Even in that journal from when I was a kid, I had visions of my true love getting down on one knee and proposing with the Eiffel Tower in the background. The ring, the white dress, the whole shebang.

But life doesn't look like those generic black and white romantic photos already in the picture frame you buy at Target, does it? That's just one, idealized moment, a snapshot. And if this whole mess has taught me anything, it's that attaching to those ideals makes all the dirty, messy, painful parts of life all that much more disappointing.

When Charm and I were planning our next trip, and he suggested Paris, I thought, *this is it. He knows this is my dream, and he's going to make it come true.* We had talked about this so much as friends that he knew how I wanted that proposal to go.

Well, you were with me, Reader, you know how all that went.

I could have been practical. I could have gotten the money back, or stashed that ticket, gone somewhere else with no associations. But that wouldn't correct the broken fairytale I was holding in my heart.

So I am going to Paris by myself. I'm taking my honeymoon alone.

Yes, I am nervous. Aside from that trip Charm and I took to the Bahamas (which is still technically the U.S.), I've never been out of the country.

And here's a side observation: The idea of me traveling alone made some people very uncomfortable. My sister asked what if I get robbed, and a lady at my church told me this horrible story about a guy who had a drink in a bar somewhere in Asia and woke up the next day with one of his kidneys missing. I was truly spooked by that one.

Remember my rant about the word "single?" Well, it's a little ironic that I've settled back into that status, and being a carefree, unattached woman in the world makes some people a little nervous. But that's probably a topic for another book.

Anyway, I did some reading, learned a little about French culture, talked to people who had actually been there. And I know it's going to be amazing. I cannot wait to walk the Champs-Elyseé, eat a fresh baguette and see the Mona Lisa with my own eyes. I'll skip the escargot.

We arrive at the airport. The car pulls up at the departure curb, and my cute driver runs to the back and sets my suitcase on the curb for me.

"Well," he smiles at me, "I hope you have a really exciting adventure!"

"I sure will, thank you!" My flight doesn't leave until 8:00 a.m., so I have plenty of time to check in, get myself a bite to eat, all that. I turn around, and the doors automatically open. And I stop cold.

6:22 A.M.

Stay Woke and Dreamer are standing right in front of the escalator, suitcases in hand. I almost drop all my stuff. "What? What are you…" I can't even get the words out.

"We're going with you!!!" They are jumping up and down, making such a racket that other travelers in the airport look over at us.

"How? What?" I cannot compute this information.

"Stay Woke and I were talking a few months ago," Dreamer explains as they both regain their composure.

"I hated to have to cancel that ticket just because Charm ditched out on you," Stay Woke chimes in.

"And I had a long talk with Mr. Dreamer, and he encouraged me to take a vacation — and who better to go with than my two best girls?"

"We couldn't let you do this alone. We had the money, we have the time, how could we not do this?" Stay Woke says. I'm about to cry, my heart feels like it's going to burst. We have a group hug, gather up our luggage and check in at the airline. I cannot believe how loved I am.

7:58 A.M.

The doors are closed. We'll be wheels up any second now. By some miracle, Stay Woke managed to get us seats together. The plane's engines hum underneath us, and we all grab hands and try to keep our squeals of delight to a minimum.

I've got my journal, and I'm determined to write it all down. This new feeling, of being free, of being alive, it shouldn't hinge on any one person, especially not a man. I can give myself this feeling! My heart is full, and I know that the next time that love comes into my life, it will be right.

In the meantime, I deserve this. I am rewarding myself for being who I am. The plane is on the runway, going faster and faster, until it lifts off. We are in the air! My dream is coming true, not because someone else made it come true, but because I did it myself.

ACKNOWLEDGMENTS

Giving honor to God, who is the head of my life!

This book is based on a real relationship I had with a man for whom I fell hard. I was crushed when we broke up, yet I believed I could get over him in ten days. So, it's only right that I first acknowledge Charm, the guy who had the leading role in the experience that changed me for the better.

To Mom: You told me to run in the opposite direction, but in true rebellion, I ran straight to him. Thank you for never judging me and allowing me to mope around the house.

To my friends, family, and anyone who supported me during the breakup and throughout the process of writing this book: I am deeply grateful for all of you.

To my sister Debbie, who encouraged me to share my idea of a "break-up" book: I appreciate you for supporting me as a blogger and now a novelist. You've inspired some of my greatest stories and been there through many of my toughest moments. Though we have our differences, we always put them to the side when it's time to have each other's back.

To Chylo, my little nugget: It's funny how the little sister can sometimes feel like the older one. Thank you for being my ride or die. I can always count on you to be there for me, to say something ridiculously funny, and to make things better—and, once in a while, worse. Life would be so boring without you!

To Bro, a man of few, yet some of the most profound, words: Thank you for being you and for always bringing light to the darkest moments.

To my awesome mentor, Sharnae: From listening to me cry to empowering me to wipe my tears and move forward, you have been there through it all. I can't begin to thank you enough for allowing me to occupy a space in your heart and for loving me as if I were your own. There isn't a day that goes by that I'm not grateful for your guidance and your mentorship.

To Sade: There are no words. How do you begin to describe the person who has been your rock? Thank you for always seeing the best in me and for promising that, "We gon' make it!" You have made sure I am always "woke." And here we are, finally on the other side of this crazy journey. I couldn't have done it without you, and I look forward to our next adventure!

To Jasmine: From living this book with me to first hearing I was going to put it down on paper, you've helped me keep my dreams alive and await my happily ever after. Thank you for being a true and loyal friend.

To Dionndra, my Mermaid Sister: You were the first person who believed in my writing. Thank you for listening to my stories and for coming along and creating new ones with me.

To Corey and Lon: Thank you for being Pastor and First Lady. You both have encouraged me to keep going on days I honestly didn't know I could. When I first shared this book idea with you, you told me you were in full support and that you'd help any way you could—as you've done with all my books. Thank you for helping me get to the finish line.

To Best: How on Earth did I wind up with a friend like you? No one should have to put up with such an obnoxious individual. Even still, when I'm in a jam, you're the one to call. Thank you for your loyalty and support. I hate you very much.

To Donny, the most creative soul I know: I can always count on you to tell me the absolute truth about any project I tackle. Thank you for encouraging me to leave Charm—and for allowing me to vent and cry on your shoulder when I went back.

To Johnathan: I appreciate your friendship. I can't believe I disliked you when we met (granted, it was warranted—*ha!*), and I'm so happy we got over our differences and became friends. You've supported me so much, you're always pushing me to go bigger in my writing, and I can always count on you to hold me accountable.

To Whitney: From reading early drafts to giving me advice on the cover so that this book could be a purple cow, thank you so much.

Thank you to Stephanie Steinberg at The Detroit Writing Room, who helped me so much through her coaching and editing. Special thanks to Dr. De'Andrea Matthews, founder of Claire Aldin Publishing, for being ever so patient. And infinite thanks to Danna, my phenomenal interior designer, and to Roberta and Erikka, the greatest cover designers I could ever imagine.

And to you, the reader: Thank you for curling up and going on this journey with me. Thank you for reading and I hope you enjoyed the ride!

ABOUT THE AUTHOR

Candace Parker is a children's book and fiction author from metro Detroit, Michigan. When she's not writing, Candace enjoys traveling, lying on the beach with her toes in the sand and satisfying her sweet tooth with a decadent brownie. Candace attended Grace Christian University to deepen her Christian faith. Her first book, a children's book called *My Vote Counts*, was released in September 2020.

www.ingramcontent.com/pod-product-compliance
Lightning Source LLC
Chambersburg PA
CBHW062225080426
42734CB00010B/2023